For the teachers, colleagues, friends and students
who have shared the walk across this modest bridge
between our two languages, English and Spanish.

INTRODUCTION TO
SPANISH
TRANSLATION

Jack Child

UNIVERSITY
PRESS OF
AMERICA

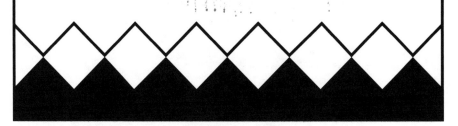

Lanham • New York • London

Copyright © 1992 by
University Press of America®, Inc.
4720 Boston Way
Lanham, Maryland 20706

3 Henrietta Street
London WC2E 8LU England

Library of Congress Cataloging-in-Publication Data

Child, Jack.
Introduction to Spanish translation / Jack Child.
p.   c
Includes bibliographical references.
1. Spanish language—Translating into English.   I. Title.
PC4498.C48   1992   428'.0261—dc20   91–47889   CIP

ISBN 0–8191–8589–2 (pbk. : alk. paper)

The paper used in this publication meets the minimum requirements of
American National Standard for Information Sciences—Permanence
of Paper for Printed Library Materials, ANSI Z39.48–1984.

TABLE OF CONTENTS

Preface

PREFACE.

This text evolved from the author's experiences in seven years of teaching translation in the Department of Language and Foreign Studies of The American University. In the Spring 1984 Semester the Department offered its first Spanish Translation course as part of its new Certificate in Translation. It soon became clear that there was strong student interest in translation and its practical application not only to language study, but also to the field of international relations, to include diplomacy, business, economics, politics, education, and communications.

The texts used in the introductory translation course varied from year to year, but no single satisfactory book or combination of texts was found. Some were too theoretical and required a strong linguistics background; others were narrowly limited to commercial or legal aspects. We collected various materials and approaches which had proven their worth, and during three trips to Antarctica and the Malvinas/Falklands Islands on a sabbatical semester in Spring 1989 wrote the first draft of this present text. It has been refined and further developed in each course offering since.

This text is designed for a third or fourth year college Spanish course. It is an introduction to the history, theory and practice of Spanish-to-English translation (there is also some consideration of English-to-Spanish translation). The emphasis is on general material to be found in current journals and newspapers, although there is also some specialized material from the fields of business, the social sciences, and literature. The 24 lessons in the text form the basis for a 14-week semester course, and each of the lessons includes brief segments on: the history of translation and the profession; introduction to theory of translation; translation problems and techniques; false cognates between Spanish and English; proverbs, idioms, and colloquial Spanish; and translation "tidbits" (brief comments on the nature of translation and humorous mistranslation).

There is also a collection of exercises (and suggested solutions) available from the author: Dr Jack Child, Department of Language and Foreign Studies, The American University,

Introduction to Spanish Translation

Washington, DC, 20016. (Tel: 202-885-2385). They are designed to allow the student to apply the translation techniques learned in each lesson as well as the false cognates, proverbs, idioms and new vocabulary. The exercises are keyed to Marion P. Holt's *1001 Pitfalls in Spanish*, 2nd edition (New York: Barron's, 1986), and to selected words from *Cassell's Colloquial Spanish* (New York: Macmillan, 1980). The proverbs and idioms are also available on a Macintosh computer program (Hypercard 2.0) with sound and interactive exercises. A syllabus for the "Introduction to Translation" course, with test materials, can be obtained from the author.

Although the author is, of course, responsible for any errors or omissions, a large number of colleagues, friends and students contributed more than their share to this project. Within the University, Department Chairs Anthony Caprio and John Schillinger were constantly supportive, as were colleagues in the Spanish and Latin American Studies group: Amy Oliver, Danusia Meson, Jeanne Downey-Vanover, Covadonga Fuertes, Frank Graziano, Pedro Vidal, Hugo Pineda, Oscar Salazar, and Diane Russell-Pineda. Lorraine Wood and Ivelisse Bonilla, as Teaching Assistants for the Fall 1988 and Fall 1991 offerings of the "Introduction to Spanish Translation" course, made important contributions to the exercises. Deanna Hammond and Ted Crump of the American Translators Association did a great deal to help bridge the gap between working and teaching translators, and consistently were available to lecture in the course and offer practical advice. Jane Morgan Zorrilla and Sally Robertson kindly provided permission to use ATA publication materials. A number of work-study assistants did much of the searching for materials: Shelly Sweeney, Dauri Sandison, Fernando Alvárez-Tabío, Nadja Reger, Kelly Bundy, Joe Clougherty, Julio Medina, Flora Calderón, Ramona Bock, Sarah Howden, and Marcela Ghiggeri. Judy Pearce provided invaluable editorial assistance.

Leslie Morginson-Eitzen, *colega, compañera y amiga*, contributed with her usual patience and understanding, as did Evita Canal de Beagle and La Perrichola. The illustrations were drawn by Daniel Neuland, and María Mactusi helped with the word processing.

Washington, November 1991.

LESSON 1: INTRODUCTION

This introductory Lesson will briefly explain the content of the six different sections you will find in each of the 23 lessons which follow.

A. HISTORY OF TRANSLATION.

The first portion of each lesson will consist of a short note on the history of translation and the development of the profession. The principal figures in the development of translation theory will be mentioned, and some of their ideas will be further developed in part C of each lesson, which deals with theory.

It is important from the beginning to distinguish between the terms "translation" and "interpretation." We will follow the usage employed by the profession, which links "translation" with the written word, and "interpretation" with the spoken word. This convention is not always followed by the media and you will frequently hear television commentators referring to "the voice of the translator," when it is in fact the voice of the interpreter you are hearing.

As will be seen in the history sections of the following 23 lessons, the history of translation and interpretation are closely intertwined. Mankind spoke before writing, and communication between tribes and nations that spoke different languages or dialects required interpretation long before their thoughts or messages were reduced to writing and thus required translation.

The history of translation and interpretation (T/I) developed in the lessons which follow emphasizes T/I in Western Europe (especially Spain), and Latin America after the Conquest. It necessarily thus ignores the equally rich history of T/I in non-European languages.

B. TRANSLATION TIDBIT.

The "Translation Tidbit" in each lesson will give you a short anecdote, horrible example, or description relating to translation. It is intended as a sort of break between the more serious sections dealing with History (Part A) and Theory (Part C).
Here is an example:
Marcy Powell tells of a Christmas card from a Chilean student that included this greeting: "May the Lord bless and can you." We can assume that the student used the first of two dictionary definitions of the Spanish word "preservar": "to can, preserve." The lesson: never trust a dictionary.
(Marcy Powell, "Traduttore Traditore," *Verbatim*, Su. 1983, p. 16).

C. THEORY OF TRANSLATION.

In this section of each lesson we will examine one or two basic theoretical concepts dealing with translation. The emphasis will be on those concepts with the greatest practical value for understanding and carrying out Spanish-English translation. The theory of translation has grown considerably in the past few decades along with advances in linguistics and communications theory. Thus, this section of each chapter can only scratch the surface of available ideas from translation theory. If you would like to explore this field in greater depth, consult the Bibliography, especially the following authors: Eugene Nida, Mildred Larson, George Steiner, Theodore Savory, J.C. Catford, and for Spanish, Gerardo Vázquez-Ayora and Valentín García Yebra.

D. TRANSLATION PROBLEMS AND TECHNIQUES.

In this portion of each lesson we will explore specific problems and techniques of some aspect of translation. There will be a mix (in no particular order) of:
- grammatical problems
- lexical (word) problems
- miscellaneous problems in Spanish-English translating

- translation for special purposes (commercial, legal, medical, etc.)
- information on the translation profession.

E. COGNATES.

This section will provide you with some of the more troublesome false cognates and partial cognates which may cause you problems in translating, especially from Spanish to English. A cognate is a word in one language which looks like, or has a similar root, as a word in a second language. Cognates may be valid ("true friends") if the spelling and meaning is identical or almost the same in both languages. Examples in Spanish-English translation would be: mapa = map; programa = program. On the other hand, the translator has to be careful with false cognates (words which look alike but have totally different meanings), such as sopa ≠ soap; ropa ≠ rope. (The notation "≠" means "does not equal"). Even more difficult at times are the partial cognates, where the two words share some meaning across the languages, but also have additional meanings in one language.

In section F of each lesson which follows, the notation "fc" stands for "false cognate," while "pfc" will represent "partial false cognate," and "pc" will mean "partial cognate." The "=" sign will mean "equals," while "≠" will stand for "not equal" (false cognate). The words in capital letters on the left are the Spanish original words, with English equivalents or false cognate definitions given on the right hand side. Where appropriate, the word will also be set in a short phrase to illustrate the meaning. Here are some examples from Lesson 2:

ACTUAL (fc) ≠ actual or real.
    = current, present: "mi hogar actual está aquí en Washington."
ADICTO (pc) = addicted to a vice
    Also = partisan or follower: "soy adicto de Menem."
ADMITIR (pfc) = to admit that something is true.
    ≠ permit entrance to a show; instead use "dar entrada."

F. PROVERBS AND IDIOMS.

In this section you will be presented with a few idiomatic expressions and proverbs from the Spanish. These are important because although they are generally untranslatable on a word-for-word basis, they usually have equivalents in English. Unfortunately, the translator must be familiar with these equivalents because any attempt to translate them word-for-word will probably result in awkward or meaningless translations.

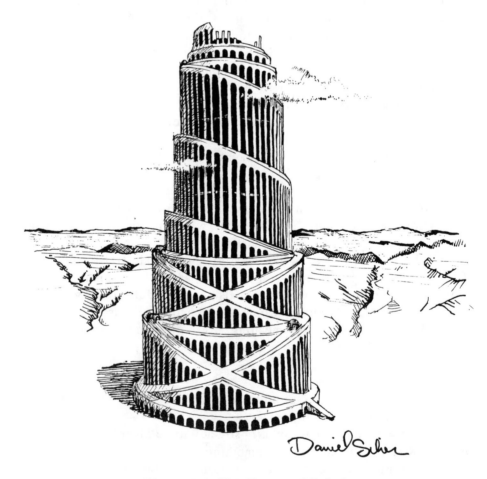

Figure 1-1: The Tower of Babel

LESSON 2

A. HISTORY OF TRANSLATION.

Translation and Interpretation in Ancient Times.

The need for translators and interpreters stems from the linguistic diversity of humankind. There are today somewhere between 3,000 and 5,000 languages spoken on earth, and from the perspective of historical linguistics the evolution of these languages is linked to the evolution of man's diverse cultures over the face of the planet. Language, after all, is the most basic expression of culture, and from a Darwinian viewpoint it would be only natural to expect languages to evolve in different directions given the different experiences each tribe or nationality experienced in a different set of geographic and cultural surroundings. But man's situation is biologically unique: in no other species are groups of that species so cut off from each other because of communication problems.

The Biblical explanation for the diversity of languages is found in the story of the Tower of Babel, as told in Genesis 11. After the great Deluge the descendants of Noah wandered onto the plain of Shinarin in Babylonia (Mesopotamia), and there in their arrogance decided to build a tower high enough to reach Heaven. An angry Jehovah punished their temerity by taking away their common language and giving them different ones, thus confusing and frustrating them since they could no longer understand each other. They subsequently scattered over the face of the earth in separate linguistic and tribal groups that account for the diversity of humanity's tongues and cultures. The etymology (word origin) of "Babel" is significant: the word Babel or Babylon is linked to both an Assyrian word meaning "gate of God," and a Hebrew root word, "balal," meaning "to confuse."[1]

Regardless of the explanation, ancient humans had a need for interpreters and translators from the first days when the different tribal groupings came into contact with each other for the purpose of

trade, diplomacy, or conquest. The Old Testament of the Bible
contains many references to the need for interpreters, for example in
Genesis 42:23 when Joseph, governor of Egypt, had to use them to
communicate with his famine-stricken Israelite brothers.[2] Although
most of the people of Biblical antiquity spoke similar Semitic
languages, Egyptian was different, and this caused a difficult
linguistic barrier. Moses, raised by the Pharaoh's daughter, drew
some of his leadership from the fact that he was bilingual in the
Egyptian and the Semitic languages, and this helped him lead the
Jews out of their Egyptian bondage.

Trade, diplomacy and military activity in the Mediterranean
Basin in ancient times required large numbers of skilled interpreters.
The ancient function of "scribe" was quite frequently associated with
that of bilingual recorder of information, with the associated skill of
translating or interpreting that information. Apparently most of these
early translators or interpreters learned their craft through travel,
contact with other cultures, or the sheer lucky happenstance of being
born to a bilingual marriage or living abroad as children (these are
still today some of the most common ways interpreters, but not
necessarily translators, acquire their basic skills). But there were
also exceptional cases when carefully selected young people were
sent abroad to learn a second language through what we today call
"immersion." In the sixth century B.C. the Pharaoh Psamtik II
created the caste of interpreters in Egypt when he sent a considerable
number of Egyptian boys to Greece to learn the language of that
country. Later Alexander the Greek ordered that some 30,000 Persian
boys learn Greek to satisfy the linguistic requirements of his
conquests, and Quintus Sertorius, who ruled Spain for eight years,
required that children of noble birth should study both Latin and
Greek.[3]

The linguists who were trained in this (and other) fashion were
frequently accorded special status as diplomats or emissaries of the
ruler. In their travels they sometimes learned the hard way one of the
occupational hazards of the translator/interpreter: when the message
is an unpleasant one, it is easy to blame the messenger. Plutarch's
Lives records that a Greek interpreter at the Persian embassy in

Athens was killed by a mob which was offended because he used the Greek language to express the demands of barbarians. [4]

B. TRANSLATION TIDBIT.

Ronald Reagan tells a story about a visit to Mexico, when he gave a speech in English to a large audience. He then sat down and a Mexican got up and spoke in Spanish. Since everyone else was applauding the Mexican every few minutes, Reagan did also. After a while the U.S. Ambassador leaned over and whispered to Reagan: "I wouldn't do that if I were you. He's interpreting your speech."[5]

C. THEORY OF TRANSLATION.

<u>What is translation?</u>

The simplest answer to this basic theoretical question is that translation is communication across the barriers posed by the Babel of different languages spoken and written by mankind. The very simplicity of this answer is deceptive. When we first learn a foreign language, we usually look for simple and direct equivalences between a thing, action or thought in the foreign language and the same thing, action or thought in our own language. At an elementary language level we can usually find these equivalences, and this is the basis of the so-called "direct translation" method of language instruction. Our teachers tend to gloss over the more subtle differences between the languages in the understandable desire to get the basic points across with a minimum of confusion. And so, since we "translate" every time we speak or write the foreign language, we get the idea that translation is simply a matter of being able to use two languages. This first experience with translation in a foreign language classroom also has the unfortunate effect of suggesting that each word in one language has an equivalent word in every other language. The resulting emphasis on "word-for-word" translation is one of the curses of the beginning translator.

The great Mexican writer (and translator) Octavio Paz has gone even further, saying that when we first learn to speak our own language, we are learning to "translate" between the world of our infantile ideas and the world of the spoken word : "Aprender a hablar es aprender a traducir; cuando el niño pregunta a su madre el significado de esta o aquella palabra, lo que realmente le pide es que traduzca a su lenguaje el término desconocido."[6]

The etymology of the word "translate" begins with the Latin root word "translatus," meaning to transfer or move from one point to another. Applied to our concept of communications, translation would then involve the movement or transfer of a message from the language we start from (we will call this the "source language," or SL) to the language we want to end up in (we will call this the "target language," or TL). The equivalent Spanish terms are "lengua origen - LO" and "lengua término - LT."

But overcoming the obstacles posed by Babel is not as simple as it looks. It turns out, unhappily, that in many cases there is no exact equivalence between words (the lexicon) in two different languages. Furthermore, at the grammatical (syntactical) level languages are different and have different ways of saying what appear to be (but are frequently not quite) the same things. And finally, there is the nettlesome problem of the idiomatic expression, metaphor or proverb which is frequently so imbedded in the culture of a language that we commit serious mistakes if we try to work at the word-for-word level. The Italians, who have had much experience with translation and its traps, sum up this problem in a neat two word cliche: "traduttore, tradittore"[7] (translator, traitor).

The translator quickly learns that he or she must inevitably make some hard choices between emphasizing the *form* (i.e., the words), and the *content* (i.e. the ideas and meaning) of the message being transferred from SL to TL. The temptation is to fall back on the words, because they are clear and identifiable. The challenge is to be sure that you have grasped the SL author's basic idea in the message and successfully conveyed that meaning in the target language in words that seem natural and even elegant in the TL.

It has been said that translation is impossible in the sense that one cannot accomplish this conveying of meaning at the same time as one is respectful of the form of the message. But translation, like politics, is the art of the possible and the necessary. The translator will have to make choices between imperfect alternatives. The purist will say that perfect translation is impossible, but it is an important human activity and must be attempted. Even if the end result is only an approximation, that approximation is better than never to have attempted the transfer of the idea from SL to TL.

Here are some other answers to the rhetorical question posed at the beginning of this section. Translation is:
- communication in the technical sense of moving a message generated by a transmitter through a communication process and channel, with distortions and noise, to a receiver.
- a decoding and coding process in which a thought in the SL is broken down into its elements, then moved into the TL through a coding procedure.
- a process of analyzing the SL message to find its deeper meaning, transfering it, then synthesizing it into the forms of the TL.
- an attempt to produce the equivalent effect on the TL audience as the thought or message had on the SL audience.
- the process by which a basic deep meaning is found beyond the words of the SL, and then ways are sought to produce the same deep meaning in the TL.

Application: the bits and pieces of translation theory we will be exploring will not make a bad translator into a good one, and there are many good translators who have never even thought about translation theory. But an appreciation of some of the theoretical underpinnings of translation will make us more sensitive to how it works (or why it didn't). Theory will also provide some guidelines for making the choices a translator is always faced with.[8] The fact that some of these guidelines suggested by theory are contradictory adds to the challenge of making the choices, and should remind us once again that translation is not as easy at it seems at first glance.

D. TRANSLATION PROBLEMS AND TECHNIQUES.

Articles, Prepositions, Pronouns and Adjectives.
    Articles: The principal problem encountered with articles is that Spanish uses them more than English. Thus, the native Spanish

speaker tends to commit an Hispanicism by overusing articles when translating into English, and the native speaker of English tends to commit an Anglicism by under-using articles when translating into Spanish. The problem is very noticeable with the definite article: "the streetcar called 'Desire'" should be translated as "el tranvía llamado 'El Deseo'" and not "el tranvía llamado 'Deseo'." "Juan apostó en el caballo número siete" should be translated as "Juan bet on horse number seven," and not "Juan bet on the horse number seven." "Man is mortal" should be translated as "El hombre es mortal" and not "Hombre es mortal." "I like books" = "me gustan los libros," and not "me gustan libros."

This type of Anglicism creates an excessively telegraphic style in Spanish which is sometimes used as a parody of the English-speaker who knows only a little Spanish, and not very correct Spanish at that: "Yo tomar avión para ir Argentina donde dar papel en conferencia."

Prepositions. It has been said that the life and originality of a language is contained in its prepositions and how they are used.[9] Differences between one language and another are often emphasized in these forms of speech (which express the relationship between other parts of the sentence), than in more standard parts of the sentence such as nouns, verbs or articles. There are relatively few prepositions, but they are used very frequently and thus the translator must be on guard against misusing them. For the Spanish-English translator the problem is compounded by the fact that Spanish has only twenty prepositions, while English has considerably more: 65, by one count.[10] Non-native speakers are frequently betrayed by subtle misuses of prepositions because there are few logical rules to govern their use. Much of the usage is simply idiosyncratic and must be learned by memorization or constant exposure and use.

The Spanish preposition "en" (which can be translated as either "in," "on," or "at"), accounts for much of this confusion. In the phrase "el libro está en el escritorio" it is not clear whether the book is inside or on top of the desk, and the correct choice will depend on additional information.

In many expressions the preposition is omitted when translating, but there are also cases where the preposition is added when translating:
"El juez miró al cuadro"   "The judge looked at the painting"
"He attends the University"   "Asiste a la universidad"
"I knew Juan"   "Yo conocí a Juan."

The English preposition "for" can be translated in Spanish as "por" or "para," generally depending on whether we are expressing cause (por) or goal (para):
"He came for his book"   "Vino por su libro"
"She studied for learning"   "Estudió para aprender"

Spanish requires the preposition "a" before verbs of motion and to indicate a person as a direct object:
"comenzó a correr"   "he began to run"
"Pedro loves Mary"   "Pedro ama a María."

Pronouns. The Spanish use of familiar and formal forms of the second person pronoun (tu/usted; vosotros, -as/ustedes). creates translation problems. Frequently, when going from English into Spanish, the translator must make choices between the formal and informal depending on the general tone of the passage. When dealing with colloquial dialogue, the translator must also be alert for regionalisms, such as the use of "Vos" in the River Plate area.

Secondary uses of pronouns can also cause problems. For example, English frequently uses the editorial "we" when the deep meaning is really referring to a different pronoun, which is the one the translator must use in going into the TL:
"the nurse said, 'let's take our medicine, shall we'," which should be translated as:
"la enfermera me dijo que tomara la medicina."

Adjectives. The position of adjectives follows general rules (English before the noun, Spanish after), but there is a small class of Spanish adjectives which can go in either location, and whose meaning will change depending on the placement:
"antigua casa"   "former house"
"casa antigua"   "old house"
"un gran hombre"   "a great man"
"un hombre grande"   "a large man."

The stressed form of the adjective is more common in Spanish than in English:

"un libro mío"   "a book of mine" (more common: "my book")
"la amiga suya"   "the friend of hers" (more common: "her friend").

E. COGNATES.

fc = false cognate   pc = partial cognate (be careful)
pfc = partial false cognate (be very careful)

ABANDONAR (pfc) ≠ to give up something completely
        = to leave temporarily: "el presidente abandonó el salón."
ACTA (fc) ≠ act.
        = formal written minutes of a meeting:
                "leyó el acta de la reunión."
        Note: for English "act" in sense of "law," instead use "ley":
                "Ley Taft-Hartley."
ACTUAL (fc) ≠ actual or real.
        = current, present: "mi hogar actual está aquí en Washington."
ADICTO (pc) = addicted to a vice.
        Also = partisan or follower: "soy adicto de Menem."
ADMITIR (pfc) = to admit that something is true.
        ≠ permit entrance to a show; instead use "dar entrada."
ADVERTENCIA (fc) ≠ advertisement; instead use "anuncio."
        = warning.

F. PROVERBS AND IDIOMS.

A caballo regalado no se le mira el diente.
        Don't look a gift horse in the mouth.
A Dios rogando y con el mazo dando.
        Put your faith in God and keep your powder dry.
A duras penas   With great difficulty.
A escondidas   Without the knowledge of; secretly; under the table.
A grandes rasgos   Briefly; in outline.
A la americana   Dutch treat.
A la carrera   On the run.
A lo largo de   Bordering; along the length of.

LESSON 3

A. HISTORY OF TRANSLATION.

Early Bible translation and St Jerome.

The Old and New Testaments represent the greatest single translation project in the history of civilization. To this day there are dedicated linguistic-religious missionaries who are devoting their professional lives to understanding the intricacies of obscure tribal languages which have no written form, with the goal of providing the tribes with the Bible as their first text.

The challenge of translating the Bible from its original Hebrew and other Semitic languages has always been a delicate one because of the religious sensitivities towards modifying the Word of God in any way. But if the challenge were not accepted, then that Word would remain inaccessible to the vast majority of converts. Thus, the challenge had to be accepted, even at some risk to the translators, many of whom endured charges of blasphemy for their efforts. More than one Bible translator was burned at the stake for a supposedly distorted translation of God's words.

Because of the heavy emphasis on God's exact words as the basis for the Bible, many early translators understandably leaned towards an excessively literal translation. That is, they translated word for word in an attempt to avoid any accusation that they were changing the Word of God. While this might have been the safer course, it frequently resulted in losing much of the meaning of the original text. As we shall see in the various theoretical sections which follow dealing with "surface versus deep meaning," this is a dilemma that plagues all translators, although it has been especially troublesome in Bible translations.

The earliest systematic translation of the Old Testament was made for the extensive Greek-speaking Jewish communities in places such as Alexandria (Egypt) and the Mediterranean generally, several centuries before the birth of Christ. As Christianity spread through that same area and the remote reaches of the Roman Empire, there was an increasing demand for translation of the New Testament into a variety of languages, beginning with Latin, but also including Syriac, Coptic, Ethiopic, Gothic, Georgian and Armenian. There was little control over many of these translations, which frequently were so literal that although they might have preserved the Word of God, they did little to meet the basic purpose of making that Word available in these other languages.

And so it came to pass that in the year 384 A.D. Pope Damasus ordered the scholar Jerome (Eusebius Hieronymus in the Latin version of his name) to begin a fresh translation of the New Testament. Although Jerome was certainly not the first, or even the best, translator of the Bible, he was the first translator who left us with a detailed and analytical written record of the mental process he went through as he translated. He was in a sense the first person to lay out a "theory of translation" and to explicitly address the eternal dilemma of the translator: Do I translate words or do I translate meaning? He approached his immense task in a systematic and disciplined way, examining the many existing translated versions of the Bible, and deciding that he had to go back to the original Hebrew and Aramaic texts in order to determine the original meaning. His solution to the translator's dilemma was to translate "non verbum e verbo sed sensum exprimere de sensu" ("sense for sense, and not word for word").[11] He also wrote his Vulgate Bible in a Latin style which would be understood by the average educated Christian of his day, and not the more elevated formal style of a classical writer or a theologian. His approach, and his clear statement of it, were courageous, and brought upon his head a storm of controversy which lasted all his career.

St Jerome's analytical approach, his willingness to be subjective, and his courage to understand and convey the deeper meaning of what he was translating have earned him the nickname of "patron saint of translators." His admonition to translate the sense of the text, and not the literal word, is a basic guideline for every translator since his day.

B. TRANSLATION TIDBIT.

From a letter written by the American diplomat Bayard Taylor commenting on the language qualifications of President Lincoln's (later Johnson's) minister to Russia from 1861 to 1869:[12]

"Ignorance of any European language, I knew, was a necessary qualification, with our Government, for a diplomatic post. I have now learned that ignorance of English is still more necessary."

C. THEORY OF TRANSLATION

Surface vs deep meaning.

A basic theoretical concept with a great deal of applicability to translation practice is the notion of surface (external) versus deep (internal) meaning. A number of specialists have addressed this idea in a variety of ways, each of which will help us understand the difference between the surface structures of a message and the deeper meaning.

Larson, for example, bases her whole approach on what she calls "meaning-based translation." Translation, she argues,[13] involves changing the form of the message from one language (source language - SL) to the appropriate form in a second language (target language - TL) *without changing the deeper meaning*. She argues that the deeper meaning can in fact be expressed in both languages, and that it is the translator's task to find that link of meaning and the way in which it can be clearly expressed. She makes the important distinction between the surface structure of language, which is carried by the words, grammar and sounds (lexicon, syntax and phonetics) of the language, and the deeper structure, which involves semantics, concepts, and meaning. If we try to deal with translation at the surface structure level, we would end up moving forms of the SL into the TL, and in the process would probably do violence to the deeper meanings. Furthermore, in moving directly from SL to TL at the surface level, we would also probably be carrying over SL cultural features and biases into the TL, which will further confuse the reader by sounding unnatural in the TL. Meaning,

Larson argues, has priority over form in translation. A diagram of her approach appears in Figure 3-1.

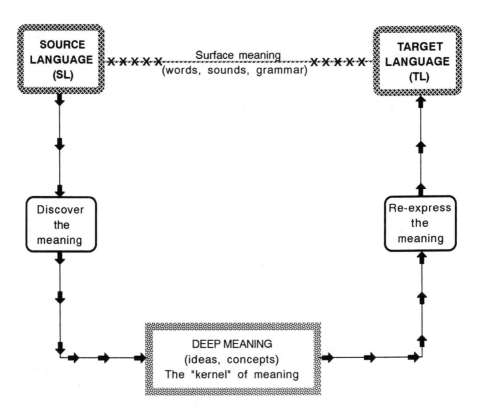

FIGURE 3-1: Larson's Translation Model

A somewhat similar approach has been proposed by the pioneering contemporary Bible translator Eugene Nida, with what he called the "coding" model. Nida argues that language (be it the written form of words, or the spoken form of sounds) originates in a concept, which is then "coded" into a language through words or sounds, respecting certain grammatical rules.[14] This being so, it should then be possible for the translator to work backwards from the source language text, decoding it through analysis to find the deeper structure, then transferring that deeper meaning into the target or receptor language by means of a coding process which reconstructs the deep meaning into the surface forms of the target language. Nida's diagram appears in Figure 3-2.

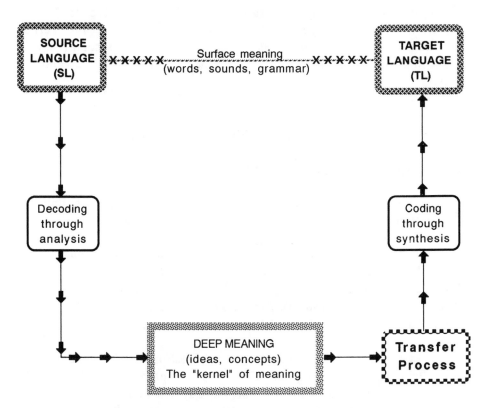

FIGURE 3-2: Nida's Coding Model

Application: Both of these approaches emphasize the point made earlier that the translator must avoid the trap of translating at the surface (word) level and instead seek the deeper meaning of the message. Here is a simple example:

English original: (context: a formal dinner) "The President raised his glass." A surface level word-for-word translation would be: "El Presidente levantó su vaso." But a translation based on a deeper meaning would proceed as follows: The context is a formal dinner in which the table settings would include goblets of wine or water. Spanish has two different words for "glass": "vaso" (meaning a plain glass), and "copa" (meaning a goblet or wine glass). In the context of the situation the deeper meaning is in all probability "copa." Further, the grammatical/ syntactical structure of Spanish would normally use the article "el" rather than the possessive "su" in a situation where each person has a wine glass. Thus, the kernel meaning is "a formal wine glass = copa," and the restructured and recoded Spanish TL translation would be: "El Presidente levantó la copa."

D. TRANSLATION PROBLEMS AND TECHNIQUES.

Business & Commercial Translation.

  This is a rich and well-studied area of Spanish-English translation, and if you would like to dig into it deeper, consult some of the following (see the Bibliography for full details):
Javier Escobar et al., *Bilingual Skills for Commerce and Industry.*
Jorge & Teresa Valdivieso, *Negocios y Comunicaciones.*
Luis Lebredo et al., *Spanish for Business and Economics.*
Ana C. Jarvis et al., *Spanish for Business and Finance.*
Louis Chacon et al., *Bilingual Business Grammar.*

  In general, business and commercial Spanish is more formal and stereotyped than English. Certain stock phrases are frequently used, and the translator should use the English ones which have an equivalent impact rather than attempt a literal translation. This is very true for correspondence, especially the more effusive and elaborate salutations and complimentary closes. Their effect if literally translated is ludicrous and must be avoided. Fortunately, the use of this type of phrase is now becoming far less frequent in Spanish, especially in the countries geographically closer to the United States. This formality in business correspondence also avoids any attempt at humor, lightheartedness or emphasis on personal relationships. The translator must be careful in going from the less formal English into Spanish, and should explain to his/her client that some changes may be required in order to preserve the equivalent impact and tone of the letter or other item being translated.

In government correspondence official slogans ("lemas") are sometimes used either in the letterhead or more commonly just before the signature block. These usually reflect an event or saying of some historical significance, and should be translated between quotation marks. The English speaking businessperson may find their use a little startling, and the translator may wish to add a brief footnote explaining the significance. Here are some examples:
"Sufragio Efectivo, No Reelección" = "Effective Suffrage, No Reelection" (Mexico; a slogan of the Mexican Revolution of 1910 against the dictator Porfirio Díaz, who stayed in power through a long series of rigged elections).
"Las Malvinas son Argentinas."
"Patria Libre o Morir" = " Liberty or Death" (Cuba).
"Nicaragua Territorio Libre de América" (During the FSLN revolutionary government, 1979-1990).
"El Ecuador ha sido, es, y será, país amazónico" (A reference to the Ecuadorean-Peruvian dispute over a portion of the Amazon Basin).

Many commercial transactions involving the government in Latin America require the use of official stamped paper ("papel sellado") of a certain type and denomination for different kinds of transactions. These generate revenue for the central government and make forgeries more difficult. The stamps generally carry serial numbers which can also be used to identify the document. Translations should include the notation "Stamped Paper, Government of _____, number _____."

Business and commerce in most Latin American countries is governed by long and complex "Códigos" (Civil, Mercantil, Laboral, as well as the Código Penal) which lay out in great detail the requirements for record-keeping, contracts, taxation, labor, working conditions, etc. This is in the tradition of the Iberian code law (as opposed to the Anglo-Saxon case law), and in fact most of these "Códigos" are similar since they originated in the Spanish colonial administration. Most of them have been translated and are a good source of terminology.

Alphabetizing in Spanish has some special characteristics which can confuse the translator (or the seeker of a number in a phone book). The letters ch, ll and rr are considered to be single letters, and words beginning with those letters are placed after the "c,""l" and "r" (not too many of these). By the same token, anything beginning with ñ comes after the "n" (there are not many words beginning with "ñ,"except in Paraguay due to the Guaraní influence). The use of the double patronymic-matronymic surname can create confusion in filing or in using the phone book. The filing sequence is patronymic-matronymic-first name, so that all the García Romeros go before the García Suárezes. Where there is a mix of single and double family names, the guiding rule is that the single ones come before the same double ones, so that all the simple Gonzálezes come before the "Gonzálezes-anything else." Examples of the sequence:

> González, Juan
> González, María
> González Pérez, Jose
> González Pérez, Ricardo
> González Suárez, Alberto

There are various ways of alphabetizing any names with the particles "de," "del," or the notation "widow of" - "viuda, viuda de, vda." Sometimes the particle is ignored and only the family name is used. In other cases all the "dels" or "de" are listed sequentially. It may be necessary to look in both places in a list or make cross-references.

E. COGNATES.

fc = false cognate   pc = partial cognate (be careful)
pfc = partial false cognate (be very careful)

AGONIA (pfc) ≠ agony in the sense of suffering intensely;
            instead use "dolor terrible."
       = usually means "dying."
AMERICANO (pfc) = "American" in sense of "Latin American" or in
            general to mean someone from the Western Hemisphere.

Usually ≠ "American" in the sense of a U.S. citizen. Instead,
use "norteamericano" or "estadounidense."
APERTURA (pfc) = aperture in the sense of hole or orifice.
Also = opening or inauguration of a formal event.
APLICAR (pfc) = to put one thing to another.
≠ request, as in "he filled out a job application":
"llenó una solicitud (o formulario) de empleo."
APOGEO (pfc) = apogee in astronomy.
Also = zenith or height of a person's powers.
APRECIAR (pfc) = to esteem.
Rarely = to appreciate.
APROBAR (pfc) = give approval.
Also = pass an exam.
ARGUMENTO (pfc) = legal or intellectual argument.
≠ disagreement; instead use "una disputa."

F. PROVERBS AND IDIOMS.

A más tardar   At the latest.
A prueba de   Proof against (water, fire, etc.)
A quemarropa   Point blank.
A quien corresponda   To whom it may concern.
A quien madruga, Dios le ayuda.   The early bird gets the worm.
A saber   Namely; that is.
A través de   Through, across.
A última hora   At the last moment; in the nick of time.
Acabar de   To have just.
Acusar recibo   To acknowledge receipt.

Figure 3-3. St Jerome, patron saint of translators.
by Albrecht Dürer, German engraver, 1471-1528.

LESSON 4

A. HISTORY OF TRANSLATION.

The Greek and the Roman approaches to translation.

These two great Mediterranean civilizations had their own idiosyncratic approaches to translation. The Greeks were somewhat ethnocentric, and with the exception of the Scriptures, they minimized the value of anything not written in Greek. Thus, although they undoubtedly learned other Mediterranean languages and interpreted *into them* in order to conduct trade, they did not translate much *from* those languages into Greek. One measure of this is the word "barbarian" (meaning "nonsense" or "incomprehensible") which the Greeks used to describe the languages of other nations. The word is apparently onomatopoeic, like the English word "babble," and suggests that the Greeks regarded other languages as inferior to their own.[15] This does not mean, however, that the great classical Greek writers were unaware of the value of translating important writings from other languages. Indeed, both Cicero and Horace commented on translation in ways not very different from those stressed by St Jerome several hundred years later. Cicero, for example, stated that a word for word translation would sound uncouth, while if he departed too much from the order or wording of the original he would not be a good translator.[16]

The Roman approach stands in considerable contrast to the Greek reluctance to translate, to the point that one writer has stated rather hyperbolically that translation was a Roman invention.[17] The great Roman enthusiasm for translation, especially from the Greek, was the result of the pragmatic Roman attitude toward the other Mediterranean cultures: if it enriched Roman culture, then it would be adopted and adapted. To do this, translation was frequently necessary, and the Roman translators became very skilled at their craft. The insertion of Greek ideas into Imperial Rome frequently meant the coining of new words in Latin based on Greek roots, and the Roman translators did not shrink from this either. At the same time the Romans appreciated the value of Latin as the great unifying tongue of their Empire for administrative, military and diplomatic purposes. The end result was that the typical educated Roman citizen was certainly bilingual and frequently trilingual: Latin was the language of administration and government, Greek the language of culture, and a third (or fourth) tongue the language of the citizen's birthplace or place of service in the Imperial system.

One of the major tasks of the translators of the Roman Empire was to render the decrees of the Roman Senate into Greek or other local languages. At the same time, translations of literature went the other direction (i.e. from Greek into Latin) as the Romans absorbed the ideas of Greek civilization. These translators had a difficult role to play, since their sophisticated readership frequently understood both the source and target languages, and would be quick to catch any errors or undue liberties. Since the typical reader had knowledge of both languages, the purpose of the translation was frequently not simply to transmit information, but to do so in ways that would express the translator's own style and ability to write creatively in his target language. This permitted the Roman translator a greater leeway than had been hitherto possible, and thus moved further away from the strict word-for-word limitations of early Biblical translation.

B. TRANSLATION TIDBIT.
From the section, "The Translator to the Reader," in the 1611 King James Bible:[18]
"Translation it is that openeth the window, to let in the light; that breaketh the shell, that we may eat the kernel; that putteth aside the curtain, that we may look into the most holy place; That removeth the cover of the well, that we may come by the water..."

C. THEORY OF TRANSLATION.
Types of translation.
        The notion of surface versus deep meaning translation is sometimes (although rather inaccurately) expressed as "literal" versus "free" translations, with "literal" being equated to word-for-

word, and "free" being translations merely inspired by the SL original, with relatively little correspondence to the words involved. There is actually a rather wide spectrum of different types of translation, which can be arrayed as follows:[19]

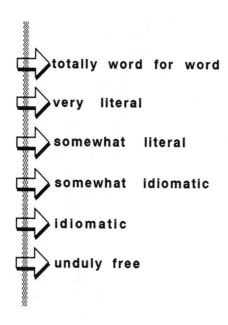

Figure 4-1: Translation Spectrum

As Larson points out, the translator should generally aim for an idiomatic translation which reads as though it is not a translation, while at the same time conveying the full meaning of the SL original. The objective is to make the TL translation sound so natural that the reader is not even aware that it is a translation. It is also possible to go beyond this into the "unduly free" category where the translator has lost or distorted some of the meaning of the SL original (or added to it).

Although word for word or excessively literal translations are usually rejected as being distortions of the deep meaning by over-emphasis on form, it is in fact possible to have word for word translations which are accurate renditions of the deep meaning. Usually these are special cases where there is a one-for-one correspondence at both the lexical and grammatical level. However, these are only valid for relatively short sentences, and cannot be relied on. When dealing with relatively simple concepts or objects that are fairly universal in nature, there is a good chance of lexical correspondence across two languages, but not if the words have special meanings associated with either of the two cultures involved. Grammatical correspondence is not uncommon when two languages are rather similar (say Spanish and Portuguese, or Spanish and French), but when the languages are different (Spanish and English) the attempt to translate too literally at the grammatical level can reduce the TL translation to awkward or unintelligible verbiage.

The Spanish words for these two terms (literal and idiomatic translation) are significant:
> literal translation: traducción servil (o literal)
> idiomatic translation: traducción oblicua (o idiomática).

The translator has another problem suggested by the spectrum above: whether to make his/her translation so pleasing and beautiful in the target language (i.e. very idiomatic) that it begins to lose faithfulness to the deeper meaning in the source language. The French express this "translator's dilemma" in terms of the beautiful/faithful nature of a lover: "Translations are like lovers: the faithful are not beautiful and the beautiful are not faithful." Another image of this type includes the idea that a translation is like the painting of a lover (the painting may be a close likeness, but it can never replace the original). The beautiful/faithful analogy is an incomplete one; actually there are four possibilities as indicated in the diagram which follows. A translation may be:
1. (B-F) Beautiful and faithful: the ideal
2. (B-U) Beautiful but unfaithful: a compromise which favors the esthetic element over accuracy and may be justified in translating poetry and literature.

3. (U-F) Ugly and faithful: a compromise which favors accuracy over esthetics, and may be justified in translating scientific, technical or commercial material.
4. (U-U) Ugly and unfaithful: the worst of all possibilities, and a situation which hopefully occurs very rarely.

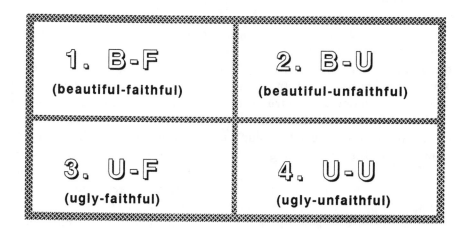

Figure 4-2: The Beautiful-Faithful Matrix

As indicated, some choices among these three (we leave out U-U) are dictated by the material involved. If we are more concerned with the esthetic qualities of literature, especially poetry, we might be tempted to take greater liberties with the deeper meaning content in an attempt to produce a pleasing or emotional effect in the TL. In contrast, if the SL material being translated is factual, engineering, scientific or commercial in nature, the tendency might be to move away from the esthetic in favor of the more strictly accurate. The descriptions "literary" and "non-literary" are sometimes used in this connection, although this is an excessively simplistic classification. A more useful classification of texts is the one suggested by Katharina Reiss:[20]
a. Informative texts (such as a scientific work, textbook, business letter); here the emphasis would be on accuracy.

b. Expressive texts (creative writing, poetry, theater), with a premium on the esthetic and emotional impact.

c. Operative texts, whose intent is to persuade (advertisements, propaganda, political speeches), and where the goal is to produce a specific reactive response. Here the emphasis may lean toward either of the two extremes, depending on the material and the circumstances.

There are some special situations in which the "word-for-word" or "very loose" extremes are called for. A word-for-word translation might be justified in an inter-linear gloss where each word of the TL is placed under its corresponding word in the SL as a guide to the grammatical structure of the SL, or as an aid in reading the SL if the reader has only a limited grasp of the SL. Partial marginal glosses are used in much the same manner in elementary or intermediate foreign language reading texts, but must be considered reading aids (much like dictionaries), and not translations. On the other extreme we have paraphrases or exegeses, where the translator attempts to put the SL into a summarized or "inspired by" version in the TL. We also have the phenomenon of excessively colloquial translations done for humorous effects, or in an attempt to make archaic material seem modern. An example would be the phrasing of a classical Greek play in 20th Century street slang.

Application: the translator needs to be aware of the spectrum of possible approaches to the TL text laid out above, generally aim for the idiomatic one, but he/she should also be prepared to shift to the other approaches when the circumstances justify it.

D. TRANSLATION PROBLEMS AND TECHNIQUES.

Letters.

The sources cited at the beginning of this section in Lesson 3 provide many samples and guidelines for Spanish commercial correspondence. For other types of letters, consult: Mary H. Jackson, *Guide to Correspondence in Spanish/Guía de correspondencia española*. (Lincolnwood, Illinois: Passport

Books, 1989.) The comment made in Lesson 3 regarding the relative formality of Spanish business writing is especially true for letters, be they commercial, personal or general. The translator must strive for "equivalent impact" so that a letter translated from English to Spanish does not sound too cold and impersonal to the Spanish reader if it follows the English too literally. By the same token, a Spanish letter translated too literally into English may sound overly effusive and bombastic.

Stock phrases may sound stilted in Spanish but generally have their English equivalents:
"Tenemos el gusto de participarle que..."
    "We are pleased to advise you that..."
"Les rogamos sirvan enviarnos..."
    "We request that you send us..."
"Acuso recibo de su amable carta..."
    "I have received your cordial letter..."
"Le ruego a Ud. tener la bondad de disculpar nuestro retraso..."
    "Please excuse our delay..."
"Mucho le agradecería se sirviera informarnos a la mayor brevedad
    posible..." "Please let us know as soon as possible..."
"Con mucho cariño, te abraza tu amigo..." "Fondly, your friend..."
"Tengo a bien solicitar..." "I would like to ask..."
"Por medio de la presente..." "By means of this letter..."
"Sírvase cancelar el pedido..." "Please cancel the order..."
"Obra en mi poder su carta..." "I have received your letter..."

One very formal Spanish manner of closing a letter is now seen less frequently, but may confuse the translator because of the variety of ways it has been abbreviated. In any case, a literal translation should be avoided. The unabbreviated form is:
"Sin otro motivo, le saluda respetuosamente su afectísimo, atento y seguro servidor." (A common abbreviation for the last portion is: "su afmo., atto., y s.s.") A literal translation would be: "Without any other purpose, your affectionate, attentive and certain servant respectfully salutes you." A more appropriate English translation would be simply: "Sincerely," or "Respectfully yours,".

Fortunately, this excessively formal Spanish style is now giving way to simpler and more direct closings which have much closer equivalents in English: "Atentamente," "Cordialmente," "De usted atentamente," "Sinceramente." Even the stock phrases such as "Obra en mi poder su amable carta de..." are being replaced by the more direct "Gracias por su carta de...."

Signatures in Hispanic business correspondence are frequently undecipherable due to the custom of adding a distinctive flourish to make forgeries difficult. These ornate signatures are more properly "rúbricas" (names written with a flourish) than "firmas" (signatures), and the translator may have no choice but to use the indication "undecipherable signature." Fortunately, the custom of having a secretary or assistant sign "for" the boss is relatively rare, and one can generally assume that the signature corresponds to the typed name in the signature block.

Junk mail is not used as much in Latin America as in the U.S., and in its place there is a considerable volume of first-class mail (usually personalized letters) promoting products or services. Before translating a large number of these, the translator may wish to alert his/her client that these are mass-produced promotional materials, and not individual personalized letters.

As an illustration of the negative impact that a poorly translated letter can make, here are extracts from two letters received in the Language Department of a major U.S. university. What is noteworthy is that the senders were companies that should have known better: one was a translation firm trying to sell a dictionary, and the second was a travel agency. The letters are an illustration of the validity of the old saying "You can buy in any language, but to sell you need to speak the other person's language."

"Dear Fellow Translator:

It is now available an up to date dictionary to cover a field that is rapidly growing in one of its more specific phases. I am talking about a dictionary of English abbreviations and acronyms in electronics, computers and industrial instrumentation, with the corresponding Spanish translation. "

The second letter:

> *"Information for:*
> *DEPARTAMENT OF GRADUATE*
> *DEPARTAMENT OF PUBLIC RELATION SHIPS*
> *DEPARTAMENT OF STUDIES OF LATIN AMERICA*

Of our consideration:

We are glad to salute you and remember you that the last february 10th we have sent you an information note about our program. ...
...
In the second fortnight of May and the first of June we will visit your country, and we would like to include or visit to you, for that we ask you to make a letter and it will be a honor and very pleased to visit you, and show you what we are prepare to do.
> *sincerelly yours"*

E. COGNATES.

fc = false cognate   pc = partial cognate (be careful)
pfc = partial false cognate (be very careful)

ARSENAL (fc) = shipyard.
≠ munitions factory;
instead use "fábrica de armas y municiones."
ARTISTA (pfc) = painter.
Also = movie or stage actor.
ASISTIR (pfc) = to help or aid (rarely); better to use "ayudar."
Usually = attend: "asistí al concierto en el Kennedy Center."
ATENDER (pfc) = to take care of.
≠ to be present at; instead, use "asistir."
AUDIENCIA (pfc) = hearing or meeting with an important person.
≠ audience in the sense of the public attending a function;
instead use "público" or "auditorio."

AVISAR (fc) ≠ advise; instead use "asesorar" or "aconsejar."
    = warn or let someone know.
BASES (pfc) = foundations.
    Also = grass roots or rank and file:
    "las bases del partido son amplias."
BENEFICIENCIA (pfc) = beneficiary.
    Also = Public Welfare Department (may also be a charity).

F. PROVERBS AND IDIOMS.

Al fin y al cabo   When all is said and done.
Al pan, pan y al vino, vino   Call a spade a spade.
Al pie de la letra   To the letter; thoroughly.
Algo por el estilo   Something like that.
Anda despacio que tengo prisa
    Make haste slowly. Haste makes waste.
Andar como loco   To run around wildly.
Antes doblar que quebrar   If you can't lick them, join them.
Antes que te cases, mira lo que haces
    Marry in haste, repent at leisure.
Buen provecho   Bon apetit.
Cada muerte de obispo   Once in a blue moon.

LESSON 5

A. HISTORY OF TRANSLATION.

<u>Spain in the Middle Ages.</u>

In the Middle Ages Spain played a vital role in preserving the culture of Western civilization by serving as a link between Christian Europe, Islam, and the Jews of the Iberian Peninsula. The Arabs had invaded Spain in the year 710 across the Strait of Gibraltar, and remained a major cultural, military and political force in Iberia until they were finally expelled in 1492. This lengthy eight century period of "La Reconquista" brought with it frequent contacts between Christians, Arabs, and Jews, and created ideal conditions for translation and interpretation between these three cultural traditions and their associated languages.

During these years Islamic culture and science were generally superior to those found in Western Europe, which had entered the Dark Ages after the decline of Rome. In the 8th and 9th Centuries the powerful Bagdad Califate had the most advanced libraries and scholars in the world in the fields of science, medicine, philosophy, philology and history, and their activities included the translation of the writings of the ancient Greeks into Arabic and Latin. The intellectual influence of these thinkers extended throughout the Muslim world, and found a special echo in the Iberian peninsula where Islam had a close contact with Christianity and the Jews of Spain. This contact was particularly notable in the city of Toledo, in Central Spain, where all three cultures were strongly represented in the Middle Ages. Toledo had been the capital of the Visigoths in Spain, but was lost to the Muslims in the year 712, and was not recovered by the Christians until Alfonso VI retook it in 1085. For almost four centuries the Arabs had made Toledo one of the great centers of their knowledge and culture, and many of the best books of Islam were to be found in Toledo's libraries. The critical mass of many scholars from the three main cultures, plus the libraries, and the tradition of intellectual and cultural tolerance, led to the creation in that city of what came to be known as "the Toledo School of Translation," or "College of Translators" in the 12th and 13th Centuries. [21]

The Jewish community in Spain played a key role in translation in these years. With their knowledge of Arabic, Latin, and the emerging Iberian romance languages, they were the principal scholars who formed the bridge between the Islamic books in the libraries and the hunger for the knowledge those books contained. The Jewish surname "Tordjman" (meaning "interpreter" in Arabic), which is still relatively common among the Sephardic Jews, is a reminder of that legacy. Maimonides (1135-1204), a Jewish scholar from Córdoba in southern Spain, was perhaps typical of this "bridging function," and he, like St Jerome, paid considerable attention to the translator's problem of word for word fidelity versus the deeper meaning of the text. In a celebrated epistle to Samuel Ibn Tibbon, Maimonides argued that any translator who attempts to simply find a single word to correspond to each word in the original language will waste much time and will produce an uncertain and confused translation. Much better, he felt, would be for the translator to understand the development of the writer's original thoughts and then express those same thoughts in ways that would be clear and understandable in the second language. [22]

The Toledo College of Translators reached its apogee under the enlightened reign of Alfonso el Sabio (1252-1284). By this time the rendering of the epic poem of El Cid into primitive written Castilian had given that language considerable intellectual prestige, and Alfonso encouraged translations of Arabic texts into Castilian, as well as Latin. The King personally took part in this enterprise; he was a scholar in his own right, specializing in lexicography as he studied ways to coin new words in Castillian to express thoughts originating in the Islamic texts.

The interest in intellectual aspects of translations in the Toledo school led them to keep records detailing the procedures by which translations were made. [23] The process involved teams of translators consisting of a Jewish scholar, who after consulting with his Islamic colleague, would read the original text aloud in Arabic and then give his version of it in Latin and the romance language (Castilian). A third member of the team, a Castilian Christian, would then (after consulting with his Arabic and Jewish colleagues) write down the version in Latin and Castilian. Since all three members of the team (Muslim, Jew and Christian) had some knowledge of all three languages (Arabic, Latin and Castilian), the process involved much discussion and debate before the final texts were produced. Doubts were resolved by consulting other translators, the rich resources of the Toledo libraries, or the King himself. Such a process would not have been possible without the overlapping presence in Toledo of rich legacies from all of these cultures and the support of the Church and King.

B. TRANSLATION TIDBIT.
From a guide book to the Basque country:[24]
"Its inheritance while humble is both subtle and penetrating in that it grasps the imagination of sensitive people and rivote ut on unspoiled frame for all the rest: its vorried vorcegated landscape of lights and shades is past the setting for a race which for so long a time has perplutated its close customs and language."

C. THEORY OF TRANSLATION.

<u>Translation and communications theory.</u>

Translation theory has drawn a number of its basic ideas from the fields of information and communications theory, which should not be surprising if we remember that we can envision translation as the coding, transfer, and decoding of messages containing information. Some of the concepts derived from communications and information theory that are useful in the field of translation have to do with things such as information load, redundancy, predictability, noise, filters, communications channels, and the need for compatibility between the transmitter, the message, the channel, and the receiver.[25]

The problem of compatibility is a basic one. Not only must all the elements involved (transmitter, channel, receiver) be ready and able to handle the message, but the message must be of a type that is expected, or at least that can be accepted by the system. Noise and filters introduce random distortions into the communication process, which must have redundancies built into the message in order to overcome the distortion. Nida notes[26] that most languages have a built-in redundancy of about 50%, which might seem inefficient, but appears to be a reasonable compromise in order to avoid the need to repeat the message if parts of it are blocked out by distortion. As an example of this type of redundancy in Spanish, we can take a simple clause: "la hermosa y simpática mujer." The redundancy here is that the female nature of the person being mentioned appears four times: in the article "la," in the "a" endings of the adjectives "hermosa" and "simpática," and in the word "mujer" itself. Other redundancies show up in stock phrases and cliches where the second portion of the cliche is so highly probable that it represents a redundancy. Thus, in the statement which begins "as cool as ..." we know from experience that there is a high degree of probability that the end of the statement will be "... a cucumber." This is built-in redundancy, and is part of the reason oral interpreters can keep up with the speaker they are interpreting.

Noise is random distortion which interferes with communications, and for the translator it is sometimes mechanical (poor print, typographical errors), or psychological, such as the predisposition of the translator or the reader in the target language to reject a concept or accept one too quickly for reasons having to do with her/his cultural background or personality. Filters have a similar effect, blocking out certain elements in a message or exaggerating the importance or value of others.

The single-language communication model can be drawn as indicated in Figure 5-1. The transmitter (person "A") begins the process by generating an idea in his/her mind. This is then coded into graphic words (if in written form) or into phonemic (sound) words if spoken. The message is transmitted via a communications mechanism or channel which must be able to accept the message in terms of format, bandwidth, and length. The message is subject to

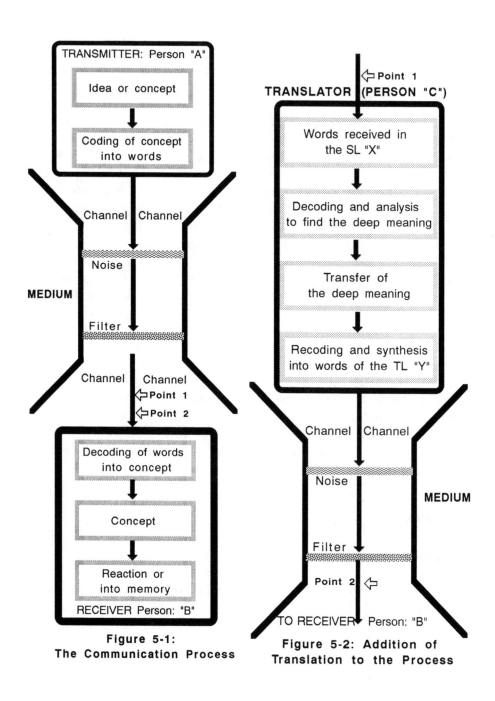

Figure 5-1:
The Communication Process

Figure 5-2: Addition of
Translation to the Process

distortions and filters in this process. Eventually it reaches the receiver (person "B") who first must decode the graphic signs or sounds into the concept, which is then processed to produce a reaction or be stored in memory.

As complicated as this process is, it becomes even more so when we specify that person "A" can only send in language "X," and that person "B" can only receive messages in language "Y." We now have to introduce a third person, "C" as the translator between A and B. The translator "C" thus becomes inserted between points 1 and 2 of Figure 5-1; see Figure 5-2 for a diagram of the translator's role. "C" receives the message from "A" via the communication channel, with all the attendant noise and filter distortions. "C" must now decode the words from "A" in language "X," determine their deep meaning by decoding and analysis, then transfer them into language "Y" by recoding and synthesizing them into words into the target language "Y." These are then transmitted through a new communication channel, with corresponding noise and filters, to the recipient "B."

Application: the communication model serves to remind us of the complexity of the translation process, and the multiple opportunities for distortions or errors to enter into the process. At the same time, an appreciation of the built-in redundancies of language helps to ease the translator's task by confirming the correctness of choice he/she has made.

D. TRANSLATION PROBLEMS AND TECHNIQUES.

Dates.

The use of slash dates in Latin America (and Europe) is different from the usage in the United States. In the U.S. the customary order is month/day/year, while in Latin America it is day/month/year. This can lead to confusion if the day could also be a month (i.e., if the day is between 1 and 12). Sometimes the confusion is eliminated by the Latin American custom of using a Roman numeral for the month, as illustrated below. In the case of a possible confusion, the translator should do whatever possible to double check, including going back to the originator of the document or text. If it is not possible to clarify by this method, then a footnote may be necessary to point out the two possible meanings to the prime reader.

    Date: 12 April 1938
    US notation: 4/12/38
    Latin American usage: 12/4/38 (possible confusion)
      or: 12/IV/38 (no confusion).

Due to standardized requirements imposed by computer formats, it is becoming increasingly common in both languages to make all date numbers have two digits, using a zero to "fill in" if the digit is a single one. Thus for the example above: 04/12/38 (US notation), or 12/04/38 (Spanish notation).

English has two standard forms of writing out dates. The more widespread is the month (initial capital), day of the month as an ordinal number, a comma, and the year: May 6th, 1989. In the military and many other government departments the standard form is: day of the month as a cardinal number, month (initial capital), year: 6 May 1989. In Spanish the equivalent standard form is: day of month as a cardinal number, preposition "de," month (lower case, but this is frequently violated), preposition "de," year: 6 de mayo de 1989. If a date is spelled out in a legal document in either language (to make falsification more difficult), it should also be spelled out in the target language.

E. COGNATES.

fc = false cognate   pc = partial cognate (be careful)
pfc = partial false cognate (be very careful)

BINOMIO (pfc) = binomial in mathematics.
    Also = linking of two names:
    "el binomio presidencial Bush-Quayle."
BIZARRO (fc) ≠ bizarre; instead use "grotesco," "raro."
    = courageous, gallant.

BRAVO (pfc) = courageous.
> Also = fierce; a person who gets mad easily.

CALIFICAR DE (fc) ≠ qualify.
> = describe as, deem:
> "lo calificó de cobarde por su falta de coraje."

CAMPO (fc) ≠ camp as in a base camp; instead use "campamento."
> = countryside, field as in playing field, football field.
> Footnote: in Anglo-Argentine slang (as well as in the Falklands/Malvinas) the word "camp" is used in English to mean "countryside."

CANCELAR (pfc): to erase or eliminate.
> Also = pay a bill or settle an account:
> "canceló la cuenta con un cheque."

CANCILLER (fc) ≠ chancellor as in prime minister of a country.
> = foreign minister. The same applies to "cancillería" = foreign ministry.

CAPABLE (fc) ≠ to be able; instead use "capaz."
> Actually, there is no such word as "capable" in Spanish, but there is a verb, "capar," which means to castrate. So "capable" in Spanish could be a neologism meaning "castratable."

F. PROVERBS AND IDIOMS.

Cada oveja con su pareja.
> Birds of a feather flock together; a mate for every old shoe.

Carne de gallina   Goose flesh; goose pimples; goose bumps.

Con destino a   Bound for.

Con las manos en la masa
> Caught red-handed. To be found with hands in the cookie jar.

Conforme a   In accordance with.

Consultar con la almohada   Sleep on it.

Contra viento y marea   Come hell or high water; against all odds.

Correr la voz   To be rumored.

Correr peligro   To take a chance.

Costar un ojo de la cara   To cost an arm and a leg.

LESSON 6

A. HISTORY OF TRANSLATION.

The Renaissance and Bible translation.

Translation played a key role in the Renaissance since the very concept of a "rebirth" of Western European civilization was based on a new look at the classics of Greece and Rome, and this required a large volume of translations from the original classical languages to the vernacular languages of Europe. The invention of printing not only facilitated this large volume of translations, but also fueled a growing demand for materials from other languages. Biblical translation was at the heart of this process, but the scope of translations went far beyond the Bible. Since the volume of translation was so great in the 14th through the 16th centuries, it should not be surprising that the quality was somewhat uneven. Some of the excessively literal translations were so close to the "word for word" approach which Jerome had warned about that they were almost unintelligible in the target language. Perhaps as a result, we can also see a growing interest in the process of translation, and an increasing interest in what we could call the "theory of translation." This interest in the process and theory of translation frequently appeared in extensive prefaces which the translator would include as part of the finished work during the Renaissance, thus initiating a tradition which has provided much of the key documentation for the history, theory and practice of translation .

A typical Renaissance statement of translation principles is that laid out by the French humanist and translator Etienne Dolet, who was tried for heresy, tortured and strangled (his body and books later being burned) because he supposedly mistranslated one of the dialogues of Plato in such a manner as to undermine belief in man's immortality. Dolet's five basic principles, as he laid them out in a brief statement ("How to Translate well from one Language into Another") in 1540, were:[27] 1. The translator must understand perfectly the content and intention of the author he is translating.

2. The translator should have a perfect knowledge of the language from which he is translating (i.e., "source language") and an equally excellent knowledge of the language into which he is translating (i.e., "target language").
3. The translator should avoid the tendency to translate word for word, for to do so is to destroy the meaning of the original and to ruin the beauty of the expression.
4. The translator should employ forms of speech in common usage.
5. Through his choice and order of words the translator should produce a total overall effect with appropriate "tone."

The religious aspects of translation in the Renaissance were focused on the need to translate the Bible into the language of the people. This had many political and linguistic implications beyond the religious ones. For one, it tended to elevate the prestige of the vernacular languages and diminish the mystique of Latin and Greek. From a political perspective, translation of the Bible into the language of the people tended to undermine the power of the Church and the function of the priests as interpreters of the Word of God. Bible translation was also intimately involved with the Protestant Reformation, which has been described as a "battle of the translators," with careers, and frequently lives, hanging in the balance if a translation was believed to promote heresy. The first English Bible translation (that of John Wycliffe, c1330-1384) was published on the premise that each Christian had a right to have access to the Word of God in his or her own language. Martin Luther's translation of the New Testament (1522) was a key document in the struggles of the Reformation and had a considerable impact on the English King James version (1611), as well as the first Spanish translations of the Bible in the period from 1543 to 1568.[28]

B. TRANSLATION TIDBIT.
From the "Guide to Lanzalote" (Canary Islands):[29] "The stones of the monument as well as the coastal segment of Arrecife are loaded with history, and when you walk through the town at tepid night, she comes towards you in unruly sensibility. During a moment, we do not know where we are; in a vilage in senorial Castilla or in a town founded by the Vice-Kings of America. Chest of Surprises that shelters in its interior the thousand years-old crab!"

C. THEORY OF TRANSLATION.

Translation process vs product.

Translation and translating involve both a product (the text that is translated) as well as a process (how you get from SL text to TL text). It is, of course relatively easy to focus on the product, and comment on translations that are good, bad, or something in between. We can establish criteria for doing this, and can identify problems in translation that cause difficulty for the working translator.

But none of this tells us very much about the process of translation. The metaphor of the computer is illustrative: most of us who use computers for word processing, number-crunching or graphics are basically concerned with what the Macintosh or PC can do, and don't really care about the programming or the inner workings. That we leave to the hackers, the designers and the technicians. What happens inside the "gray box" of María Macarena Manzana Mactusi (our Macintosh IISi) is not as important to me as knowing that if I put something in I will get a certain something out.

The analogy to translation is valid. We feed in a message coded in the SL and we get out a message coded in the TL. Somehow the "black box" of the translation process in between the input SL and the output TL manages to switch from SL to TL. We know that for a quality translation this switching is accomplished at the deep meaning ("kernel") level rather than at the surface level of word, sound, style and grammar, but just how this happens is something of a mystery to us.

It should be a comfort to hear that the best theoreticians in the translation field are also mystified about what happens in the switching mechanism inside the "black box." Here is Nida's opinion: "We actually do not know precisely what takes place in the translator's mind when he translates, for psychologists and neurologists do not know the manner in which language data are stored in the brain. The fact that in some brain injuries the capacity of bilingual persons has been reduced to the speaking of one language and not the other has led to the belief that there might be compartmentalization in the brain. However, this hypothesis has been generally rejected."[30]

We can elaborate somewhat on our "black box" by saying that the input function involves comprehension and is relatively passive, while the output function involves expression (writing) and is active. These functions are linked by a switching mechanism which, if the models of Nida and Larson are valid, involves stripping the input SL text to its deep meaning, then finding the equivalent way of expressing that deep meaning in the TL text. This is the switching process which is still a mystery. Once we switch, then we shift into the active expressive writing mode and produce the TL output text.

Figure 6-1: The "Black Box" Model

We can draw three practical lessons from this model:
1. The success of an effective input function depends on comprehension of the SL text. There is no particular need to be able to write, speak or produce in the source language: understanding is the important thing. Understanding is far more than the words; we must understand the context and the culture in which the text is imbedded. To do so we need to study everything we possibly can about the SL culture, even at the expense of being able to speak or write the source language itself.
2. The success of an effective output expression function lies in being able to write well in the target language. The output text should be not simply understandable, it should be natural, idiomatic

and free-flowing. The translator should thus do everything possible to improve her/his writing skills in the TL.

3. Unless a translator is extraordinarily gifted, there is little chance he/she will be able to write naturally and idiomatically in anything but his/her mother tongue. Thus, translators are well-advised to stick to translating *into* their native tongue. There are exceptions to this, and sometimes job responsibilities require it. Translating into a second or third language can also be a useful tool for learning that second or third tongue. But to stake your reputation as a translator on your ability to write well in that second or third language is a risky business.

Specialists have made many suggestions for improving the translation process. They include having a wide and almost encyclopedic range of knowledge, as well as depth in the specific field you are translating in. There is also the factor of motivation and the translator's attitude toward the text and the original author. Ideally, you should enjoy and respect the text you are translating, and feel that your effort will result in other readers enjoying (or profiting from) that text as well. In the real world the translator's motivation is frequently money, although few people make a living exclusively as translators. Exercising the translation switching mechanism is also a creative process, with all the satisfaction that any creative process brings. If the process also serves your ideals, ideology or religious beliefs, then the sense of purpose and satisfaction is magnified. This perhaps explains why the Bible remains the largest translation project undertaken by man, and why religious translators are so motivated and satisfied by their efforts.

We close this section with a set of twelve rules or guidelines frequently given to translators. Their contradictory nature may seem to eliminate their usefulness, or suggest that this whole exercise is a joke, but it was presented quite seriously by Savory[31] to indicate that the translator frequently has to make difficult choices. The twelve instructions, adapted from Savory's presentation, are:

Words vs ideas:
1. A translation must give the **words** of the original.
2. A translation must give the **ideas** of the original.

Impression upon reading:
   3. A translation should read like an **original work**.
   4. A translation should read like a **translation**.

Style:
   5. A translation should **reflect** the style of the original.
   6. A translation should **possess** the style of the translator.

Time setting:
   7. A translation should read as a contemporary of the **original**.
   8. A translation should read as a contemporary of the **translator**.

Omissions and additions:
   9. A translation **may** add to or omit from the original.
   10. A translation **may never** add to or omit from the original.

Poetry:
   11. A translation of verse should be in **prose**.
   12. A translation of verse should be in **verse**.

Application: It all depends. The translator's job is to make the right choices. The translator has to nurture and develop his/her "black box" to maximize the comprehension of the input and the expressivity of the output.

D. TRANSLATION PROBLEMS AND TECHNIQUES.

Capitalization and abbreviations.

   The translator will encounter some idiosyncrasies in each language which may cause problems in handling capitalization and abbreviation (including acronyms).

Capitalization.

   Spanish tends to capitalize less than English does. Some of the items which are not capitalized in Spanish, but are capitalized in English, include:

- Words in a title of a book, article or play. Spanish, of course capitalizes the initial word, but not the others: "Gone with the Wind" = "Lo que el viento se llevó."
- The personal pronoun "yo/I."
- Months, days of the week.
- Adjectives of nationality or race.
- Names of languages and races of people.
- The first word of each line of poetry (except the first line). However, when translating poetry in bi-lingual editions, the convention is to follow the pattern of the source language.

From an orthographic point of view, if a word carries a written accent in Spanish on its initial letter, that accent should also be present if that word is capitalized. However, for typographic reasons the accent is usually not placed on a capital letter because the end result would be to make the accent spill over onto the line above. Some typographers will use an accented capital letter in a smaller size font to make the letter fit on the line.

Abbreviations and Acronyms.

These can cause the translator a surprising amount of difficulty, and anyone writing an original text which might be translated should keep this in mind when drafting the text.

It is important that the translator not blindly leave the abbreviation in its original form without knowing what the source language abbreviation meant, or being sensitive to what the same letters might mean in the target language. The classic case which is often cited[32] involves the Spanish abbreviation "TM" ("toneladas métricas") and the English "TM" ("tons per minute"). If the translator leaves the Spanish TM as "TM" in English, this happens:
Source language: 100 TM de carbón (i.e., 100 toneladas métricas)
Target language: 100 TM of coal (i.e., 100 tons per minute).

An example with contemporary political implications for inter-American relations involves the letters "CBI." To American diplomats these letters stand for President Reagan's "Caribbean Basin Initiative," but in Spanish they are associated with "Conflicto de Baja Intensidad" (English: Low-Intensity Conflict - LIC), which is the current jargon for guerrilla and counter-insurgency warfare.

There are some words which can be abbreviated in the source language, but not in the target language. In this case the word must be written out in the TL if there is a chance of misunderstanding:
Washington, D.C.: Washington, Distrito de Columbia
Buenos Aires, DF: Buenos Aires, Federal District
fdo. Juan Ramírez: signed Juan Ramírez

Spanish requires a period at the end of all abbreviations, while English does permit some to be used without a period (mph, mpg). Spanish uses a double letter to indicate that an abbreviation is in a plural form; when using this double letter form the period comes after the second letter, not after each letter:
USA = EE. UU. de N.A. (for "Estados Unidos de Norteamérica")
R.R. ("railroads") = FF.CC. ("ferrocarriles").

There are no firm rules for translating acronyms, and the translator needs to keep her/his target audience, or "prime reader," in mind. The translator must frequently make hard decisions regarding acronyms. Sometimes the SL acronymn has penetrated the TL in its original form and is used as such, even though the words can be translated when spelled out:
"The CIA denied it..." = "La CIA lo negó..."
"The Central Intelligence Agency denied it..." =
    "La Agencia Central de Inteligencia lo negó..."

In other cases the acronym deals with an international organization which regards each language as official, and thus an acronym exists in both languages: UNO=ONU; OAS=OEA.

The more difficult situations are when the translator does not know if the prime reader will be familiar with the acronym. For example, this Spanish SL phrase dealing with Argentine presidential candidate Carlos Menem of the Partido Justicialista:
SL: "El candidato presidencial del PJ, Carlos Menem..."

We can leave the acronym in the original, assuming the reader will know what it means: "The presidential candidate Carlos Menem of the PJ..."
Or we can write out the acronym in the SL by way of explanation: "The presidential candidate Carlos Menem of the PJ (Partido Justicialista)..."
Or we can write out and translate: "The presidential candidate Carlos Menem of the PJ (Partido Justicialista-Justice Party)..."
Or we can write out, translate and explain: "The presidential candidate Carlos Menem of the PJ (Partido Justicialista-Justice Party of the Peronistas)..."
What we do not have the license to do as translators is to simply create an acronym that is not in TL usage: "The presidential candidate Carlos Menem of the JP..."

Spanish acronyms have no written plurals and use no periods. The gender of the acronym is derived from the full written form:
La CIA is feminine because it is "la Agencia Central de Inteligencia."
El SIDA (AIDS) is masculine because it is "el síndrome de imuno-deficiencia adquirida."
El FBI is masculine because it is "el Buró de Investigación Federal."
There are some exceptions to this rule due to accepted usage and euphony.

E. COGNATES.
fc = false cognate   pc = partial cognate (be careful)
pfc = partial false cognate (be very careful)

CARPETA (fc) ≠ carpet or rug; instead use "alfombra" or "tapete."
    = folder, as in file folder: "las cartas están en la carpeta."
CASUALIDAD (fc) ≠ casualty as in hurt person;
    instead use "baja," "víctima."
    = coincidence, chance: "nos encontramos de pura casualidad."
CATEDRATICO (fc) ≠ associated with a cathedral.
    = tenured professor at a university.
CHARLATAN (fc) ≠ quack or phony doctor;
    instead use "curandero" o "médico falso."
    = talkative; one who pretends to be more than one really is.

COLEGIO (fc) ≠ college as in university-level institution; instead use "universidad."
= secondary school, usually private.
COLLAR (pfc) = collar of a shirt.
Also = necklace.
COLORADO (fc) ≠ colored (for an expression such as "people of color," use the phrase "gente de color").
= red. Also "ponerse colorado" = to blush.
COMPROMISO (fc) ≠ agreement; instead use "acuerdo, convenio, solución equitativa."
= commitment, date, obligation.
CONCENTRACION (pfc) = concentration.
Also can = mass meeting or rally, especially a political one.

G. PROVERBS AND IDIOMS.

Cruzarse de brazos   To be indifferent.
Cuanto antes   As soon as possible.
Cuentos verdes   Off-color jokes; "blue" jokes.
Cuesta abajo   Easy; downhill.
Dar a luz   To give birth.
Dar de baja   To discharge; to drop from a team or unit.
Dar en el clavo   To hit the nail on the head.
Dar gato por liebre   To deceive; to cheat.
Dar las gracias   To thank; be grateful.
Dar mucha pena   To be very sorry; to be very embarrassed.

LESSON 7

A. HISTORY OF TRANSLATION.

Translation/Interpretation in the Discovery and Conquest.

The impact of translators and interpreters in the Renaissance was not limited to literature. This was also the Age of Discovery and the Age of Commerce and Trade, when Europe burst out of her historical borders with unparalleled energy, enthusiasm and curiosity into the world beyond. The contacts with a bewildering range of new civilizations and languages in the New World, Africa and the Far East placed a severe demand on the translators and interpreters available to the merchants, missionaries and explorers who carried the dynamism of the Renaissance to distant shores. Columbus, for example, included among his crew in 1492 a few men who knew Arabic because he believed that the Arab traders had already reached Cipangu and the Spice Islands (Columbus' destination), and he felt that Arabic would be a language through which he could communicate with the inhabitants of the lands he would reach. We know the name of one of Columbus' interpreters: he was Luis de Torres, and was typical of those Hispanic Jews who had been so effective in the bridging of linguistic gaps between Arabic, Hebrew, Latin, and the vernacular languages of Iberia. Columbus was not able to use Luis de Torres, of course, but upon his return to Spain he brought back with him six Indians with the idea that they were to learn Spanish and thus serve as interpreters in future expeditions.

Magellan too carried interpreters, and he took pains to buy slaves at his various destinations who would serve to help him communicate. On board Magellan's ships was a remarkable Italian, Antonio Pigafetta, who kept the historical record of the expedition as well as a sort of running vocabulary of the various languages they encountered.[33] These included the Tupi-Guaraní tongue of South America, and Pigafetta's work served as the foundation for the linguistic work done by the Jesuits among the Guaranis several centuries later. Pigafetta was also the recorder of exotic new life forms found in the New World, including the first reference to penguins (from Southern South America) in European writings.

The Catholic Monarchs, Ferdinand and Isabel were well aware of the significance of language and translation. The year 1492 was not only the year of Columbus and the fall of the last Moorish bastion of Granada, it was also the year that Elio Antonio Nebrija of the University of Salamanca published his basic grammar of the Castilian language, which did much to establish Castilian as the dominant language of what was fast becoming the nation-state of Spain. As this language established its dominance over the Peninsula, Nebrija's *Gramática de la Lengua Castellana* was carried by the conquistadores, missionaries and educators to the New World as the model for translating the Indian tongues into Spanish. As the Bishop of Avila put it when he presented Nebrija's *Gramática* to the Queen in 1492, "language is the perfect instrument of empire."[34]

The close links between the Castilian language, the Roman Catholic religion, and the Spanish Conquest can be seen in the process known as the "requerimiento," drawn up by King Ferdinand and his advisors. The Spanish Crown stipulated that in their first contact with any new groups of Indians the Conquistadores had to read them the "requerimiento," which was a demand that they peacefully accept the Catholic Church and the authority of the Crown of Castile and Aragon. If after having heard the "requerimiento" they refused, then the conquistador had the right to impose himself by force. The obvious problem was one of languages: the Crown stated that interpreters must be available to present the "requerimiento" to the Indians in their own tongue. In order to obtain such interpreters, the first conquistadores in the early years of the 16th Century made forays to the mainland of the Aztec Empire to capture Indians who would then be forced to serve as linguistic bridges between the Castilian of the conquerors and their native tongues.

Another source of interpreters for the early conquistadors were shipwrecked Spaniards who had lived among the Indians. The most famous of these was Jerónimo de Aguilar, who stayed with the Mayas of Campeche (the Yucatán Peninsula of Mexico) for eight years before being rescued by Hernán Cortés. As we shall see in the next lesson, Aguilar was to play a key linguistic role along with Marina/Malinche in the conquest of the Aztecs.

However, the Maya learned by Aguilar was not the language of the Aztecs, the major empire of Middle America. The Maya civilization had declined markedly by the time of the Conquest, although its language was still spoken in the area which is today Guatemala and adjoining Mexico. The Aztec empire was centered on the city of Tenochtitlán (today's Mexico City), and the Aztecs spoke Nahuatl. In fact, the widespread use of Nahuatl was a key element which bound together the Aztec empire, consisting of a series of tribes under the control of the Mixtecs in Tenochtitlán. They, like the Catholic Kings of Spain, also realized that "language is the perfect instrument of empire." Although each subordinate tribe could retain its own language, the Aztecs insisted on imposing Nahuatl as the official language of the empire, and trained their own linguists, as well as members of the conquered tribes, to be scribes in the Nahuatl language. To achieve a position of importance in political, military or commercial activity in the Aztec empire, it was essential to speak Nahuatl.[35]

B. TRANSLATION TIDBIT.
Sign in a posada in Chinchón, Spain:[36]
"Will we must say you tomorrow morning we haven't warm water till 11 hours to 15 hours. Thanks you."
"Les comunicamos que mañana día 21 de Mayo, no tendremos agua caliente desde las 11 de la mañana hasta las 3 de la tarde."

C. THEORY OF TRANSLATION.

Translation, language, and culture.

Language is arguably man's greatest and most sophisticated cultural achievement. Perhaps the one thing that most distinguishes *homo sapiens* from other species on earth is the ability to express thoughts in words, to transmit those words through sounds or written symbols, and pass them on to other human beings far away in time and space. We consider culture here in the broad sense of the sum of those socially conditioned parts of man's behavior which each human being must learn (as opposed to those parts which are instinctive or hereditary). Each human being grows up in a culture in which s/he learns his or her language, and that language is conditioned and imbedded in that culture. The naming of things, thoughts, and actions is accomplished with reference to the specific culture in which the child grows up. The specific language of a person's community, with all its quirks, habits, style and nuances, are what give us our first language, and form the lens or filter through which we learn all subsequent languages.

This explains why translation should not be thought of so much as a transfer between languages, as a transfer between **cultures**. The two languages cannot be separated from their parent cultures without risk of losing meaning. By extension, the translator who works effectively with deep meaning below the surface features of two cultures must be bicultural as well as bilingual.

Larson[37] explores the problem at the basic level of lexical mismatches between cultures (there are, of course, much more complex mismatches dealing with syntax and style). To take a simple example, it would appear that the concept of a "house" as a place to live in would be universal across all cultures. And in fact, all languages have a word which captures the deep meaning of "house" as a place to live in. But the word has a different meaning and mental image for a middle-class suburban American, for example, than for a nomadic llama-herder of the Bolivian Altiplano. And so the expression "to be on the roof of your house" makes sense for the American, but not for the Bolivian who lives in a small and fragile tent made of animal furs.

Here are some examples from Spanish-English translation:
The translator may be tempted to render the English word "hospital" as its apparently valid Spanish cognate "hospital." But in Latin America "hospitales" are generally charitable institutions used by the poor; members of the upper middle class and the rich go to private "clínicas." Thus, the choice of the transformation into either

"hospital" or "clínica" depends on the specific meaning, and requires that the translator know the cultural and sociological difference.

"Friday the 13th" would be translated as "viernes 13" if it were simply a matter of dates; to connote the sense of a bad luck day, it would have to be "martes 13."

For countries in the tropics seasonal differences are not as important as rainy and dry seasons. In fact, in the tropics the rainy season is usually called "invierno" and the dry season "verano," regardless of when they occur. So how, then, does one translate "she goes to school in the summer"? The reversal of seasons in the northern and southern hemispheres creates another problem, as can be seen in translating "un caluroso diciembre," since it means something quite different if one is in Washington or Buenos Aires.

Finally, how does one translate terms such as "bear market," "to check," "baby-sitter," "dumping," "hobby," "pet," "licenciado," "Bogotazo," "cátedra," "caciquismo," "caudillo," "junta," "foco," "campesino"?

At this point one is tempted to despair over the possibility of any meaningful translation between different cultures. Indeed, if one accepts that language is deeply and inextricably bound up in the parent culture then translation is in fact impossible. On the other hand there is an equally extreme view that holds that culture affects language only at the surface level, and that at the deep meaning or kernel level we are dealing with common concepts. The trick in translation then, is to find the equivalent surface structures in the two languages which correspond to the common deep meaning.

A more reasonable intermediate position would hold that the degree to which a satisfactory translation is possible depends on how deeply and uniquely imbedded a particular idea is in a particular culture, as well as the distance between the two cultures we are translating. Nida[38] cites four fundamental factors in the human experience which make communication and translation possible (although not always fully satisfactory). These include: 1) the similar mental processes of all human beings; 2) the similar physical responses to the same emotional stimuli; 3) the range of common cultural experience; and 4) the capacity of man to adjust to and understand the behavioral patterns of others.

In a time of mass communication which transcend cultures, it is useful to conceive of the culture-language relationship as being partly common to all of humankind, and partly specific to one's own smaller linguistic community. Even when *homo sapiens* lived in small, isolated cultural communities there were still shared concepts, such as male/female, hot/cold, food and animal/human, as well as verbs describing actions, and expressions for present, past and future time. As mankind evolved and communications between cultures increased, these concepts were increasingly shared, although they may still have nuances of meaning in different cultures. But given the homogenizing impact of mass communication, the trend seems to be toward fewer translation problems stemming from culture-bound ideas and words.

For the translator there are of course devices for solving the problem of bridging the gap across cultures, providing that the translator is culturally aware of the differences. The translator can, for example, explain the conceptual differences in a footnote or in the text itself. It also possible to coin or borrow a word from the SL into the TL as a neologism; indeed, the lexicon of a language frequently grows through the translation process in this manner.

In dealing with the relationship between language, culture and translation, we must also address the issue of artificial languages, such as Esperanto, which are not imbedded in a culture as other languages are. This lack of a cultural base goes a long way toward explaining why such languages have difficulty being accepted and do not grow in a dynamic way as other languages do. They have a "cultural" base in the sense that a common body of human beings interested in promoting international understanding support the artificial language, but their use and growth are obviously artificial and limited, and cannot be considered in the same category as languages with a traditional cultural foundation.

Application: The translator ignores the cultural base of the SL and TL at his/her peril. The translator has to be aware of the special significance that all terms, even universal ones, can have in different languages.

D. TRANSLATION PROBLEMS AND TECHNIQUES.

<u>Advertising Translation.</u>

The translation of advertising copy is a topic of considerable interest from both a commercial as well as a cultural perspective. Such translation is essential in order to get U.S. products into Spanish-language markets (in the U.S., Latin America and Spain), as well as to promote products from Spanish-speaking countries in the United States. Bilingual airline in-flight magazines contain some of the best (and worst) examples of this genre of translation, and their errors or effectiveness are glaringly evident because they are usually printed in both languages on opposite pages. The very word for "advertising" poses a false cognate problem since the corresponding Spanish word is "propaganda," which has other connotations in English. The apparent Spanish cognate for advertising ("aviso") means a written ad, and not the broader concept of advertising.

In some ways the problem of translating advertising copy is similar to the translation of poetry or dramatic works because of the special use that advertising makes of language and extra-linguistic factors such as layout, color, symbol, images, and myth. Advertising copy is deeply rooted in culture and folklore, with traps of double meanings and unintended jokes, perhaps more than almost any other kind of material a translator may encounter. For this reason the use of native speakers, and specifically those native to the sub-cultural group being targeted for the ad, is essential. To violate this rule is to run the risk of having an ad be counter-productive. Not only should the translating be done by a native speaker, but the resulting copy should be tested in a representative sample group to look for effectiveness and possible booby traps.

In the United States the Hispanic market[39] has traditionally been considered to include four major groups: the Hispanics of Mexican descent in the Southwest (in turn these can be divided into the "Old" Hispanics who have lived here since the Spanish conquest, and the more recent arrivals from Mexico); the Puerto Ricans; the Cubans (in several distinct waves of migration); and finally a last category which would include all the others. Each of these groups, and their numerous subgroups, shares the common language up to a point. In their slang and colloquial Spanish there are considerable differences, and it is at this level that advertising copy must operate. In some of these groups the names for foods and other common objects are quite different. There are also vulgar and sexual innuendoes and double meanings for certain objects, such as varieties of fruits. Further, many Hispanics live in a double culture, and advertising copy in Spanish may not reach them. Fortune Magazine[40], for example, notes that these include "Chuppies" (Chicano urban professionals) and "Yucas" (young upwardly mobile Cuban-Americans); they are described as "confusing as hell. They drive BMWs and watch network TV. But they live with Cuban grandmothers and listen to salsa radio." The U.S. Army found that its ad campaign targeted at young Hispanics (who watch TV in English) was not as effective as putting it on Spanish-language TV because that age group still went to their parents (who primarily watch Spanish-language TV) for advice on career choices.

The premium in advertising translation is on high-quality, hard-hitting copy with maximum effectiveness. The information load in the medium is very high, and is conveyed by many factors besides the lexicon. It is also a high-risk proposition, as can be seen below from some of the examples of counter-productive advertising. The possibilities of cultural mismatch are high, and can easily result in the ad being ignored or, worse yet, becoming the butt of jokes.

The advertising translator has a number of other problems. If the copy is being translated for a major U.S. firm that does not specialize in the Hispanic market, the senior executives of the firm are not likely to know or understand the Hispanic market or the Spanish language. But they will see the Spanish ad and, equipped with perhaps a vague memory of their high school Spanish, may question the ad because it doesn't sound like or look like the English ad it was translated from. The translator, working closely with the layout specialists, must also be concerned with "copy fit" (the way the written part of the ad meshes with the graphics and the total layout). Because Spanish tends to need more words to deliver the same message, this can frequently cause problems. If the translation is for an ad to appear in another country, the translator working for an advertising firm must also be aware of legal implications. References to the competition, for example, are now permitted in the U.S., but may not be in other countries. Likewise, there may be certain requirements for mandatory information on the package, such as for tobacco products. While these are not strictly translation problems, the translator may get involved as an advisor on cross-cultural and international aspects of marketing and advertising.

Despite these problems, the interest in effective use of translation to put ads into the Hispanic market will continue to be high. It is estimated[41] that by the year 2015 Hispanics in the U.S. will number 40 million and will surpass blacks as the country's largest minority group. At present the earning power of Hispanics is well over $50 billion per year, with a disproportionately high percentage of that amount being spent on essentials such as food and clothing. Hispanics watch considerable amounts of television, and have a high degree of brand loyalty, especially if there is a feeling that the brand is culturally attuned to their wants and needs.

Here are some classic mis-translations of advertising copy:[42]
- Braniff's ad telling Hispanics they can fly "en cuero" (the intent was to bring attention to Braniff's leather seats, but "en cuero" means "naked").
- The use of the word "bichos" in a pesticide ad promising that their product would kill all kinds of "bichos" (the problem is that "bichos" can also refer to male genitals).
- Morris the cat talking about his nine lives; (in Hispanish folklore cats have seven lives).
- Frank Perdue's boast that "it takes a tough man to make a tender chicken" came out with a double meaning in Spanish that "it takes a sexually aroused man to make a chick affectionate."
- The following extracts from a California county government form:
    "¿Estar usted interesado en a bajo interés préstamo componer o añadir a tu casa? Si así, por favor completo esta forma y traer a City Hall en la franqueo pagado sobre no mas que viernes, cuatro de marzo, 1983."
- And finally, this survey question: "El jefe de la casa es de Spanish/Hispanic origin o decente?"

E. COGNATES.

fc = false cognate   pc = partial cognate (be careful)
pfc = partial false cognate (be very careful)

CONFECCIONADOR (fc) ≠ confectioner as in pastry-maker;
    instead use "confitero."
    = maker or drafter in a general sense: "confeccionó el tratado."
CONFERENCIA (pfc) = conference (rarely);
    instead use "congreso, entrevista."
    = lecture or formal presentation.
CONFLICTO (pfc) = (rarely) conflict as in war.
    Usually = difficult situation, strain.
CONSTIPADO (fc) ≠ constipated in the bowels;
    instead use "estreñido."
    = to have a cold.
CONTACTO (pfc): usually = physical contact.
    Generally ≠ to be in communication;
    instead use "comunicarse con."
CONVENIENTE (fc) ≠ convenient in the sense of comfortable.
    = advisable, necessary: "no es conveniente ir a la guerra."
CONVICCION (pfc) = conviction as in beliefs
    ≠ conviction as in sentence; instead use "condena."
COPA (pfc) = goblet or prize cup: "the ship won the Americas Cup."
    ≠ coffee cup; instead use "taza."
COPIA (pfc) = reproduction or imitation of an original.
    ≠ copy of a magazine or book; instead use "ejemplar."

F. PROVERBS AND IDIOMS.

Dar parte To inform; to report; to invite to an important occasion.
Dar una mano To apply a coat (of paint); to help out.
De acuerdo con In accordance with.
De dirección única One-way.
De etiqueta Formal dress.
De golpe Suddenly.
De Guatemala a Guatepeor From bad to worse.
De hecho As a matter of fact.
De la noche a la mañana Overnight; in a short time.
De mal en peor From bad to worse.

LESSON 8

A. HISTORY OF TRANSLATION.

Hernán Cortés and Marina/Malinche.

The Conquest of Mexico is a prime example of the psychological as well as linguistic contribution which can be made by translators/ interpreters. Upon arriving on the Mexican mainland at Veracruz, Cortés discovered that his main interpreter Jerónimo de Aguilar was initially of very limited use to him since he spoke only Maya, and the dominant language as they entered the Aztec empire was Nahuatl. However, Cortés' fortunes soon changed when the chief of the Tabasco tribe gave him an Indian maiden in tribute. The woman's name was originally "Malintzin" in Nahuatl, but she was known as "Malinche," and eventually "Marina" in the Hispanicized version. She had been born into a powerful family, but after her father died her mother remarried and bore a son to her second husband. She favored the boy, and in order to permit him to get her inheritance she got rid of Malinche by selling her to the chief of Tabasco. Malinche thus spoke Nahuatl as well as the Maya language of the lowland tribes. By pairing up Jerónimo de Aguilar and Marina, Cortés now had a team of interpreters through which he could speak to the Aztecs and the tribes dominated by the Aztecs who had been forced to learn Nahuatl. Cortés would speak to Aguilar in Spanish, Aguilar to Marina in Maya, and Marina to the Aztecs or their subordinates in Nahuatl. Today we would call this process "consecutive relay interpreting," and while it is not especially elegant or efficient, it did permit communication. Cortés' chronicler, Bernal Díaz del Castillo, noted that when Malinche joined the group their great conquest could finally begin in earnest. [43]

But Malinche was soon to become more than a cunning relay linguist. She also became Cortés' lover and advisor, sharing with him the secrets of the Aztecs which gave him a psychological edge over his opponents. As the intimacy of their relationship unfolded, Cortés taught her Spanish, and once she could communicate with him directly in this language, there was no further need for Jerónimo de Aguilar: Cortés could now talk to the Aztecs in Nahuatl through the direct simultaneous interpretation of Malinche, who was now increasingly being known as "Marina" and eventually "Doña Marina." One of the most famous drawings of Malinche/Marina shows her standing between a group of Aztecs and a group of Spaniards, with the Aztec hieroglyph for "word" (a curl sign shaped like a comma) flowing in both directions between the Aztecs and Spaniards, but through Marina/Malinche. The drawing captures the essence of the task of the simultaneous interpreter.

Marina interpreted for Cortés in his dealings with the Aztec emperor Montezuma, and Montezuma thought so highly of her that he began to refer to Cortés as the "lord of Malinche." It is also probable that Marina provided Cortés with key insights into the mind of Montezuma, explaining to him the Aztec legend of Quetzalcoatl which held that some day a powerful king would arrive, and that this king would be pale of skin and white of beard. Cortés matched that description, and used this information to break down Montezuma's resistance.

On numerous occasions Marina was able to provide the Spaniards with "intelligence information" which allowed them to launch preemptive attacks or avoid ambushes. In Cholula, for example, the wife of one of the chiefs trusted Malinche, and revealed to her that the Cholulans were planning to ambush and assassinate the Spaniards. Marina passed this information on to Cortés, who captured the leaders of the plot and had them killed.

There is a tragic side to the story of Marina/Malinche. Although Cortés had great respect for her linguistic ability and fathered a son (Martín Cortés) by her, he also regarded her as something less than his wife, and in fact "gave" her to some of his fellow conquistadores for their enjoyment as a mistress.[44] Among Mexicans to this day "malinchismo" is an insulting term applied to those who sell their birthright to foreigners.

B. TRANSLATION TIDBIT.
Sarcastic comment on translators by the 17th Century British poet
John Denham:
"Such is our pride, our folly and our fate,
That only those who cannot write, translate."

Which suggests the following, equally invalid:
Those who cannot do, write.
Those who cannot write, translate.
Those who cannot translate, teach translation.

C. THEORY OF TRANSLATION.

Translation and linguistics.

If translation is a science, its scientific base will be found in
the field of linguistics. Linguistics systematically studies languages,
and a number of its subfields offer interesting possibilities for the
translator seeking explanations for some of the problems s/he
encounters. Semantics, for example, deals with the relationship
between referents (linguistic symbols such as words, expressions,
phrases) and referends (the concepts or objects to which they refer).
The importance of semantics for the translator derives from the
Larson-Nida models of the translation process (Lesson 3) and the
relationship between deep meaning and surface meaning. Translation
could thus be described as the process by which the linguistic
symbols (referents) in the source language are probed to find the
deep meaning referends, which are then linked to the target
language's own linguistic symbols.
Sociolinguistics deals with the social registers (or social levels) of
language and the problems of languages in contact with each other in
a geographic region. The applicability of this subfield of linguistics
to translation will be explored in Lesson 18.
Semiotics, or the scientific study of signs, is relevant to the
translator because words are signs, and the pragmatic process of how
they become attached to the concepts they are linked to has relevance
for the process of translation.

The relationship between translation and linguistics can be further illustrated by the classification of types of translation proposed by the linguist Roman Jakobson:[45]

1) Intralingual translation or *rewording* is an interpretation of verbal signs by means of other verbal signs in the same language. Example: shifting the register or level from convention to slang, as in "It is all right" to "It's OK."

2) Interlingual translation or *translation proper* is an interpretation of verbal signs by means of some other language. Example: from English "It is all right" to Spanish "Está bien."

3) Intersemiotic translation or *transmutation* is an interpretation of verbal signs by means of nonverbal sign systems. Example: from English "It is all right" to the handsign circle made with the thumb and index finger. Caution: if you make this sign meaning "OK" in certain Latin American countries, you may achieve a somewhat different result, illustrating that semiotics also has links to the cultural base the sign is imbedded in.

The translator should be aware that modern linguistics is a relatively new science, with still unresolved contradictions among several major approaches. As Schogt has put it:[46] "Quite often a translator turns for help to linguistics in order to solve a specific problem he has encountered in his work, frequently to be disappointed as he does not receive the help he expected. Instead of providing a nice elegant solution to a particular translation problem, the linguist he consulted gives him reasons why there is no solution or offers him a choice of approximate equivalents that he could have found without any outside help. Theories of translation include many elements of a linguistic character, however, and linguistic theories are part and parcel of translation handbooks."

Application: Even at its present stage of evolution, linguistics has made important contributions to understanding and carrying out translations. In the sections that follow we will be using some of these applications in terms of comparative linguistics and the specific translation techniques of modulation, transposition, addition, and omission.

D. TRANSLATION PROBLEMS AND TECHNIQUES.

<u>Interjections, Expletives, Euphemisms and Regionalisms.</u>

Interjections and expletives. These are grammatical particles and single words used to express subjective reactions such as fear, pain, excitement, astonishment, and anger. They are also sometimes used as "fillers" in spoken speech, where they may add force to the statement being made, but do not contribute any other meaning. Exclamation marks usually set them apart from the rest of the sentence or paragraph, and in Spanish the upside-down exclamation mark must precede the interjection or expletive if one is used after it. Some interjections and expletives are quite regional, and are either unknown in other regions, or have a different impact. Spanish frequently uses religious names and terms (Dios, Jesús, María, Virgen, Santos) to express these emotions in ways that do not translate well into English, and the translator must be careful to select equivalents with the same force.

Here are some of the more common Spanish interjections and expletives, with English equivalents:
¡ah! (for admiration, sorrow, surprise) = oh!
¡ay! (for pain, sorrow) = oh!
¡bah! (for disgust, bother, repugnance) = bah!
¡caramba! (for annoyance, astonishment) = wow! shoot! gee!
¡ojalá! (for a wish or hope) = I sure hope so! would to God!
¡puf! (for disgust, bad smell) = phew!
¡uf! (for disgust, annoyance) = ugh!
¡vaya! (for annoyance) = come, come!

Euphemisms are softer or more agreeable terms used in place of words which are offensive, repelling, taboo, or which instill fear or bring bad luck. They are used in written and spoken speech to cover a delicate matter, vulgarity, unpleasant truth, or an indecency. At the folk level euphemisms may be commonly used to avoid bad luck or to prevent a superstition from coming true. At upper socio-economic levels they are employed to avoid seeming crude or vulgar, and they sometimes verge on hypocrisy. Euphemisms can be created by changing the form of the original word, replacing it with another, using a foreign word, or otherwise coming up with a generally accepted substitute. Charles Kang's *Dictionary of Spanish-American Euphemisms* contains the following categories:

Superstition: words for "Devil," names of animals, diseases. The Evil Eye. Physical defects, death, killing.

Delicacy: family relationships, forms of address, occupations, age, physical appearances.

Mental and moral defects: stupidity, insanity, anger, scolding, lying, avarice, drunkenness.

Financial status: poverty, wealth, money, debts.

Offenses and consequences: stealing, fleeing, playing truant, jail, policeman, beating.

Decency (the body): bodily odors, underwear, belly, breasts, posterior, sex and sex organs, bodily excretions.

Decency (love): Concubine, prostitute, "mentar la madre," pander, brothel, effeminacy, coition, onanism, pregnancy, giving birth, cuckold.

One set of euphemisms with parallels in English and Spanish are words generated as expletives based on excretion. This accounts for a series of Spanish expletives beginning with the letters "ca...," while English, for the same reason, has numerous expletives beginning with the letters "sh..." These words have different force, and can be graded along a scale from the definitely crude to the mild and acceptable in polite company.

Euphemisms for sex and private body parts are numerous, and frequently vary from region to region. Fruits, vegetables and other objects which might conceivably bear a resemblance to a sex organ are frequently used as euphemisms, and may be misinterpreted. The prime reader who runs into these words may believe that the text has a sexual double meaning when none is intended. Words that are acceptable in one country may be insulting or vulgar in another.

In translating interjections and expletives, the important point is to achieve the same equivalent impact on the prime reader as was achieved in the source language. Because of the shades of meaning and regional differences involved, the translator should be careful in dealing with these words, and should consult a native speaker with good regional vocabulary to verify the appropriateness of the translation. In the absence of such a native speaker, use *The Insult Dictionary* and *Cassell's Colloquial Spanish Dictionary*.

Regionalisms. A number of regional Spanish dictionaries are available for words which exist only in certain regions, or which have different and possible embarrassing meanings in certain countries. For example, in the River Plate area the verb "coger," which is perfectly acceptable in Spain and much of Latin America, has sexual connotations and usually must be avoided. Its use by unsuspecting translators or foreigners has often led to snickers, laughter and embarrassing situations, such as those described in several issues of *Verbatim (The Language Quarterly)*.[47] Similarly, the word "calentura" can mean "fever," or "sexual excitement," with predictably different results if used carelessly. In Mexico, to be "constipado" means to be congested in the sense of having a cold, while in South America the cognate (meaning "congestion of the bowels") is valid. Bennaton tells the story of a Mexican delegate at an international conference who mentioned that he used Vicks when he had a cold ("uso Vicks cuando estoy constipado") but his remark was rendered by an Argentine interpreter as "when I am constipated I use Vicks." There was apparently some astonishment over this novel medical procedure.

E. COGNATES.
fc = false cognate   pc = partial cognate (be careful)
pfc = partial false cognate (be very careful)

CRIATURA (fc) ≠ creature in the animal sense.
    = baby or infant.
CORRESPONDIENTE (pfc) = corresponding in sense of parallel.
    ≠ newspaper correspondent; instead use "corresponsal."
CRIOLLO (fc) ≠ creole, as from regions of Louisiana.
    = of Spanish descent but born in Latin America, or "local."
CUESTION (pfc) = question as in theme or subject.
    ≠ question as in interrogative; instead use "pregunta."
CURSO (pfc) = a series of events.
    Generally ≠ a course of study at a university;
    instead use "asignatura" or "materia."

CINICO (fc) ≠ cynical as in skeptic, negative;
　　instead use "escéptico."
　　= shameless, irresponsible: "se desempeñó como un cínico."
DECEPCION (fc) ≠ deception in the sense of lying or hiding;
　　instead use "engaño."
　　= disappointment: "sufrió una decepción cuando perdió."
DEMANDAR (pfc) = to sue in a court of law.
　　Generally ≠ "demand" in the sense of strongly requesting;
　　instead use "exigir."
DESGRACIA (fc) = disaster, tragedy, misfortune.
　　≠ disgrace in sense of shame; instead use "vergüenza."
DESHONESTO (fc) ≠ dishonest in sense of not being honest;
　　instead use "no es honrado."
　　= immodest, lewd, indecent.

F. PROVERBS AND IDIOMS.
De memoria　By heart; memorize.
De pura casualidad　By chance.
De tal palo, tal astilla　A chip off the old block.
Dejar a uno en la calle　To bleed white; to rip off.
Dejar a uno plantado　To stand someone up.
Del dicho al hecho hay mucho trecho
　　There's many a slip 'twixt the cup and the lip.
Desde luego　Of course.
Dicho y hecho　No sooner said than done.
Digno de confianza　Reliable.

LESSON 9

A. HISTORY OF TRANSLATION.

The Conquest of Peru and El Inca Garcilaso.

Like that of Mexico, the Conquest of Peru involved translators/interpreters in important ways, although Francisco Pizarro never had the good fortune to encounter a single individual so compelling as Marina/Malinche. On an early voyage to the New World Pizarro brought two young Indians (Martín and Felipillo) from Panama back to Spain to be taught Spanish and converted to Christianity. Both were involved in Pizarro's encounters with the Inca King Atahualpa, and history suggests that their incompetence or deliberate misinterpretation caused problems.

The most dramatic incident was the "requerimiento" laid before Atahualpa. The priest in charge of explaining Christianity and the power of the Spanish King to Atahualpa was Father Vincente de Valverde, an arrogant and inflexible man. Whether because of poor interpretation or his own pride, Atahualpa rejected the requerimiento and threw the Bible which Father Vincente handed him to the ground. This provided the Spaniards with the excuse they sought to seize him and demand ransom for his release. His interrogation was handled through the Indian interpreter Felipillo, who managed to mislead and confuse both the Spaniards and Atahualpa with his poor interpretations. One explanation was Felipillo's poor knowledge of both Atahualpa's Quechua (which of course was not Felipillo's native tongue), as well as Spanish. A more sinister explanation[48] is that he belonged to one of the subordinate tribes that hated the Incas, and furthermore, that he had fallen in love with one of Atahualpa's concubines and feared for his life if Atahualpa should remain in power. Atahualpa was executed by the Spanish, but Felipillo also came to an unhappy end: he got caught up in the civil wars between the various Spanish conquistadores of Peru, deserted Pizarro for his rival Diego de Almagro, and was eventually hanged.

A happier symbol of translators/interpreters in the Conquest of the Inca Empire of Peru is the much admired figure of El Inca Garcilaso de la Vega (1539-1616), who symbolically carried in his veins the blood of Spanish conquerors and that of Inca royalty. He had the good fortune to receive an education from the Spaniards as well as the oral traditions of his Inca ancestors on his mother's side. As a result he was a "bridge" person between the two cultures, well qualified to interpret each side to the other, both from the cultural aspect as well as the linguistic one. He has been given credit for both persuading his Inca countrymen to accept the inevitability of the Conquest, as well as attempting to smooth some of the harsher aspects of the Conquest imposed by his Spanish cousins.[49] He was also the first American-born writer who earned a well-deserved reputation in Spain as well as his native Peru. He went to Spain at an early age, and there drank deeply of the heady spirits of Humanism and the Renaissance. He began his literary career by translating into Spanish the "Dialoghi D'Amore" by León Hebreo, and then (as a member of the expedition), he wrote an account of Hernando de Soto's adventures in Florida. But his masterpiece was the *Comentarios Reales de los Incas* in which he chronicles the best that the ancient civilization had to offer before it was disrupted and destroyed by the Spaniards. He writes as an "interpreter" in the broad sense of the word, trying to explain the ways of the Incas of his mother's lineage to the Spaniards of his father's. The work is a linguist's delight, since he sprinkles it with Quechua words and explains these to his Castilian audience. He includes poetry in trilingual versions; here is a brief example which includes the Quechua original, the classical Latin, and the Castilian of the Golden Age:

Inca (quechua)	Latin	Spanish
Cumac ñusta	Pulchra nimpha	Hermosa doncella
Toralláquim	Frater tuus	aquese tu hermano
Puyñuy quita	Urnam tuam	el tu cantarillo
Paquir cayan	Nunc infrigit	lo está quebrantando
Hina mántara	Cujus ictus	y de aquesta causa
Cunuñunun	Tonat fulget	truena y relampagea.

B. TRANSLATION TIDBIT.

From the program for the opera *Carmen* in the Genoa Opera House:

"ACT I. Carmen is a cigar makeress from a tobago factory who loves with Don Jose of the mounting guard. Carmen takes a flower from her corsets and lances it to Don Jose. (Duet: "Talk Me of my Mother"). There is a noise inside the tobago factory, and the revolting cigar makeress bursts into the stage. Carmen is arrested and Don Jose is ordered to mounting guard her. But Carmen subduces him and he lets her escape."[50]

C. THEORY OF TRANSLATION.

Comparative linguistics: Spanish and English.

The most useful subfield of linguistics for the translator is comparative linguistics, which looks at the lexicon, phonetics, grammar, and stylistics of two or more languages on a comparative basis. Comparative linguistics studies ways in which two languages are similar as well as different, and in the case of differences, can suggest the closest equivalent structures or words. The value of such an approach to the translator is obvious, since this analysis will tell him or her what forms can be appropriately used in making the transfer from SL to TL.

As many comparative linguistics scholars (such as Vázquez-Ayora) have pointed out, English tends to be concrete, direct, and descriptive, with a relatively fixed word order. As a language, it is especially well suited for science, technical information, and business. Spanish, on the other hand, is more abstract, affective, and indirect, with a much more flexible word order. Thus, it is more suitable for poetry, for love, and for elegant or dramatic discourse.

English has been described as moving more comfortably in the concrete plane of reality, while Spanish feels more at ease in the abstract plane of the intellect or emotion. English sees the world in descriptive terms, while Spanish in affective ones. English presents a series of "snapshots" of reality while Spanish is more concerned with how that reality affects people. English has many word images and slang terms which efficiently summarize reality in its most concrete form. Spanish is more subjective, examining the effect that nature and reality have on the observer. English has a simple 5-form verb structure, while Spanish has an extraordinarily complex one (46 different forms), with a heavy emphasis on the subjunctive to express shades of meaning, emotion and intention. English has a simple past tense, while Spanish plays with the differences between preterite and imperfect to indicate whether the action is specific and short term, or continuing. English has the simple verb "to be," while the Spanish "ser/estar" provides many nuances of transitory states of emotion or permanent inherent characteristics. Further, the translator must grapple with whether the simple English "you" should be rendered as the formal Spanish "Usted" or the more intimate "tu."

A number of specific and practical situations stemming from comparative Spanish-English linguistics will be dealt with in Section D ("Translation Problems and Techniques") of each lesson, but some of the general categories with examples will be given here as illustrations. English has a tendency to use the passive voice much more than Spanish, which relies on the reflexive ("se") instead. Although employment of the passive voice in Spanish is not wrong, its excessive use will sound strange to a native speaker, who will get the feeling rather quickly that the text is an excessively literal translation from English. Adverbs are not as commonly used in Spanish as English. Frequently an adjectival or verb clause is a more natural translation in Spanish for an English adverb. Example:

He complied happily   =   Cumplió con mucha alegría

Since Spanish is a more emotional and affective language than English, many interjections, especially ones involving the invocation of God or other religious figures, must be toned down somewhat in English to avoid an exaggerated sense of emotion. In business letters the customary effusive Spanish salutations and endings must likewise be reduced to shorter and less emotional English formulas.

The English usage of many nouns as adjectives gives it an especially efficient and dense aspect, whereas Spanish does not

permit this and must frequently either generate new adjectives or explain the concept in a roundabout manner. Some examples:
labor-intensive industry =
    industria que emplea gran densidad de mano de obra
commuting = traslado diario entre el domicilio y el trabajo
antiestablishment = contra el orden establecido
forcible transfer = traslado de carácter obligatorio
input-output device =
    dispositivo para la entrada y salida de datos informáticos
co-loan = préstamo cofinanciado
desk officer = funcionario especializado en un país
shotgun methods = métodos empíricos aproximativos
tanker = buque cisterna
background paper = documento de información básica.

There are exceptions, however, where Spanish is more efficent and specific:
aftosa = hoof and mouth disease
pagaré = promissory note.

Comparative linguistics sometimes makes clear that there simply is no lexical equivalent between two languages because of the culture in which they are imbedded. This often happens when technical or scientific progress is made in one culture, which generates words to match the needs of those advances. The second language may not have any such equivalents available. In such circumstances the translator may attempt to insert a neologism he/she has coined, or may be forced to go into lengthy circumlocutions to describe the new concept. In other cases a culture may have a rich variety of words to describe an important or frequently occurring phenomenon (snow among skiers, bananas in the tropics, penguin varieties in the Antarctic), but the second language may have only one general word to cover the whole category. Folklore within a culture tends to create many types of constructions which fall into the category of "metalinguistics" (i.e., beyond linguistics) such as word-plays, puns and other idiosyncrasies which may or may not have fairly close equivalents in the second language. These will be examined in greater detail in the Lesson on idioms and metaphors which follows.

Application: The translator should take advantage of the comparative linguistic work done between Spanish and English to gain a deeper understanding of the similarities and differences between the two languages, as well to pick up specific translation techniques.

D. TRANSLATION PROBLEMS AND TECHNIQUES.

Proper Names, Places, Titles, Punctuation.

These categories can cause some confusion for the translator, since the rules are complex and there are exceptions.

Proper names. In general, the names of people are not translated. "John Smithson" does not become "Juan Hijo de Herrero." However, the names of kings are frequently translated, especially into Spanish, if the name has an obvious equivalent in the TL. The names of saints usually do have such equivalents, and are translated. So are the names of some major historical figures that have equivalent forms (some rather different): Alexander the Great- Alejandro Magno; Archimedes-Arquímides. The Pope is the only living person whose name is always translated. Religious, military, professional and other titles (such as those indicating nobility) usually have a version in the TL, which should be used, but always keeping in mind the principle of equivalent impact. Sometimes using the translated term creates an awkward situation and a different impact. For example, in Latin America many professions use titles linked to names, such as Ingeniero Juan González, Abogada María Pérez, Arquitecto Samuel Trinka. To render these titles with their English equivalents sounds odd and probably should not be attempted unless necessary for the full meaning of the text. Where no English equivalent is known (e.g., for "Licenciado," or "Don") the SL original may be used, or it may be omitted, depending on the situation.

Geographic names. These follow no particular pattern. The prevailing tendency is to not translate, especially if the name is not widely known in the TL. However, if it is a well-known place name which has a euphonic problem in the TL (i.e., it sounds awkward), then it may very well have its own form in the TL: London-Londres; New York-Nueva York. Sometimes the change is in the spelling: Brasil-Brazil; Spain-España. Sometimes place names are translated if they have descriptive meaning: República Dominicana-Dominican Republic; (but El Salvador is not translated as "The Saviour," nor Costa Rica as "Rich Coast"). Within Mexico the capital is usually referred to as "México," but outside of the country the usage "Ciudad de México" or "Mexico City" is employed to avoid confusion. If the geography is politically sensitive (usually because of competing claims), there may be different names in two languages, and these must be handled carefully to avoid problems. Whether one says "Islas Malvinas" or "Falkland Islands" makes a political statement, especially if the speaker takes the trouble to say "Islas Malvinas" when speaking in English or "Falkland Islands" when speaking in Spanish. In attempting to remain neutral some analysts use the double terminology "Malvinas/Falkland Islands" or "Malvinas (Falkland) Islands" or, as the U.S. State Department did during the 1982 conflict: "the South Atlantic islands located at longitude... and latitude..." The translator must keep both the intent of the original author and the needs of his/her prime reader in mind when approaching a problem of this type. Street names are generally not translated, although the descriptive word ("street" or "avenida") normally would be. Plazas or squares are generally not ("the mothers of the Plaza de Mayo").

Titles of works. These are usually translated, unless there is some over-riding reason not to, such as a word-play or double meaning in the original language. One strongly-made suggestion is to let the translation of the title wait until the very end to be sure that some deep meaning assigned to the SL title is not overlooked[51.] Titles can be very tricky, and an effective translation of a title can take many hours of thought, or be the product of a brilliant flash of insight. Titles of long diplomatic reports, which seem to be especially prevalent in international organizations, cannot be changed much without offending someone's sensitivities, and the end result usually is long and ungraceful: "Report of the Special Commission to Study the Inter-American System and to Recommend Measures for Restructuring It."

Punctuation. One important difference between Spanish and English punctuation is the use of the initial (upside down) question mark and exclamation sign. Spanish **must** have them, and when going from English to Spanish the translator sometimes encounters difficulties in knowing where to put the initial Spanish sign. Another difference is that English places the period and comma inside the quotation marks in direct quotes, while Spanish puts them outside: He said: "well done." but "Dijo: "bien hecho". (For consistency in this book we are employing English usage). The translator frequently uses quotation marks in the TL to indicate an unfamiliar word, a neologism, or a word used outside its normal meaning. By so using the quotation marks the translator brings this term to the reader's attention as being unusual. Example: compró "software" muy interesante para su computadora.

E. COGNATES.
fc = false cognate   pc = partial cognate (be careful)
pfc = partial false cognate (be very careful)

DISCUTIR (pfc) = to argue.
    Generally ≠ "discuss," but is sometimes used this way.
    Instead use "intercambiar ideas," "platicar," "hablar."
DISGUSTO (fc) = displeasure, argument, difficulty.
    ≠ disgust in sense of repugnant; instead use "dar asco" or
    "asqueroso."
DORMITORIO (pfc) = dormitory of an institution.
    But also means "bedroom" in a home.
DROGUERIA (pfc) = drug store, but is more, since a "droguería"
    sells a number of other items.
    "Drug store" = "farmacia" or "botica."
EDITOR (fc) ≠ "editor" of a newspaper; instead use "redactor."
    For a book editor, use "compilador."
    A "casa editorial" is a publishing house.
EDUCADO (pfc) = well-mannered: "los niños bien educados."
    Generally ≠ has a good education;
    instead use "tiene una buena formación."
EFECTIVO (fc) ≠ effective; instead use "eficaz" or "eficiente."
    = in cash: "pagó la cuenta en efectivo."

ELEMENTAL (pfc) ≠ elementary; instead use "rudimentario."
= dealing with the elements.

F. PROVERBS AND IDIOMS.

Dime con quien andas y te diré quien eres.
A man is judged by the company he keeps.
Dios mediante   God willing.
Dirigir la palabra   To address, to talk to.
Día hábil   Workday.
Don de gentes   Charisma; way with people.
Donde hubo fuego hay cenizas.   Where there's smoke, there's fire.
Donde menos se piensa salta la liebre.
The unexpected always happens.
Echar a perder   To go to waste; to spoil (as in fruit, or children).
Echar de menos   To miss, feel the absence of.

Figure 9-1. Marina/Malinche interprets, standing between the
Spanish on the left and the Aztecs on the right.
Source: Codex Florentino, around 1540.

LESSON 10

A. HISTORY OF TRANSLATION.

Translation/interpretation in the Colonial period.

The linguistic policy of the Spanish Catholic Monarchs Ferdinand and Isabel required that their possessions in the New World be "Castilianized" as soon as possible. Having established their Iberian power base partly on the unifying force of the Spanish language, they extended this concept to the Americas and called for teaching their new Indian subjects the Castilian language. The main responsibility for this task was given to the "encomenderos," who were those Spanish conquistadores to whom large numbers of Indians were granted ("encomendado") for the purpose of converting them to Christianity and teaching them Castilian in return for the use of their labor. In practice the Indians' labor was exploited by the encomendero, but the Christian conversion was very nominal and the teaching of the Castilian language minimal.

An alternate solution for communicating with the Indians existed, but was not used much. That solution involved using the existing and widespread "linguas francas" in the Americas: Nahuatl, Maya, Quechua, and Tupi-Guaraní. The Aztecs had built their empire at least partially on the strength of the common language of Nahuatl. A similar phenomenon existed in the Inca empire, where the power structure was based on forcing the tribes which were subjected to Inca rule to learn the official Quechua language. The descendants of the Mayas in Guatemala and much of Central America still spoke that tongue even though the Mayan cities had disappeared into the jungle by the time the Spaniards arrived. Although there was no similar "Guaraní empire," this latter language was in widespread use in the broad South American region extending from the Paraguayan Chaco and Southern Brazil to the River Plate. The strength of these four languages can be illustrated by the fact that in large areas of Latin America to this day, these languages are still spoken and in fact are the dominant tongues in rural areas of Mexico, Guatemala, Bolivia,

Peru, Ecuador, and Paraguay. Had the Spaniards taken the trouble to systematically learn these four languages (Nahuatl, Maya, Quecha and Tupi-Guaraní), they would have been able to directly communicate with the vast majority of their new subjects. But with rare exceptions (most notably among the missionaries) this did not happen, and the conquistadores and their followers relied basically on the use of mestizo Indian interpreters to act as intermediaries in the dealings between the Castilian-speaking Spanish administrators and merchants, and the Indian masses.

In the Vice-royalty of New Spain (roughly today's Mexico, Southwestern United States and Central America) this gave rise to a group of interpreters/translators known as "naguatlos." Typically they would be mestizos who had insights into both cultures (Spanish and Indian) as well as both languages. They were frequently the only Indians who could write, and were trained by the Spanish to be court translators, record-keepers, legal secretaries, and sometimes minor government officials at the village or municipal level. They also had another characteristic: a capacity for cunning and deception which the Spaniards had taught them to use in dealing with the Indians. The naguatlos, and their counterparts in the other areas, frequently played the Spaniard off against the Indian, using their knowledge of both languages as their principal tool.[52]   At times the deception involved simply keeping a part of the taxes levied from the Indians, and telling the Spaniards that the Indians had refused to pay their full tax. At other times they falsified records to their advantage, cheating both the Spanish and Indians.

The principal exception to this arrangement of using native translators/ interpreters was the system instituted by the Christian missionary orders. Under the strong influence of the work of the grammarian-historian Antonio de Nebrija, the Spanish religious authorities in the missionary orders stimulated the study of the principal native tongues, and encouraged their priests to write formal grammars of these languages (modeled on Nebrija's *Gramática de la Lengua Castellana*), so that the gospel and other religious materials could be taught to the Indians in their native languages.[53] At the same time this allowed the missionary priests to preach in the native languages without having to depend on sometimes unreliable and even deceptive translators/interpreters such as the naguatlos.

B. TRANSLATION TIDBIT.
From a regulation posted at a hotel in Jalisco, Mexico:[54]

"There won't be more than two people on each bed. If the guest requests it the Administration can install aditional beds. It is understood that no guest will keep in his room other person without been registered at the Administration."

"No se admitirán más de dos personas en cada cama. A solicitud del huésped la Administración podrá instalar camas adicionales. Queda entendido que ningún huésped podrá alojar en su habitación a otra persona sin antes haberla registrado en la Administración."

C. THEORY OF TRANSLATION.

Modulation.

Modulation is a translation technique suggested by linguistics and translation theory. It tells the translator that he/she should "shape" (or modulate) the text as it is being restructured into the target language so as to make it sound more natural in the TL. The word "modulate" means to regulate, to arrange, or to shape. In radio communications theory, the concept of modulation refers to the way in which the basic high-frequency radio wave is shaped in order to carry the lower-frequency audio wave of the human voice or music. Thus, in amplitude modulation (AM), the amplitude or size of the peaks of the high-frequency radio wave are modified so that the lower-frequency voice or music audio is carried on the tips or peaks of the radio-frequency wave. In frequency modulation (FM) it is the frequency itself which is modified to carry the audio by increasing or decreasing the frequency of the radio wave to correspond to the changing pitch of the voice or music.

In translation, modulation relies on shaping the structure somewhat as it is transformed into the target language in order to give it an idiomatic "feel." It does not work with syntax and grammar as much as it does with symbols and cultural referents of the target language. Modulation does not change the meaning of the concept being translated, but changes the way it is expressed using different symbols (words) than the SL does. Some examples:

The ambassador suggested a carrot and stick policy.
El embajador sugerió una política de pan o palo.
        (Not "zanahoria y palo").
Bolivia es un país mediterráneo.
Bolivia is a land-locked country.
        (Not "Mediterranean").
El Canciller pidió la palabra.
The Foreign Minister asked for the floor.
        (Not "the chancellor"; not "the word").
It was the opinion of an armchair politician.
Fue la opinión de un político de café.
        (Not "un político de sillón").
It was a massive lobbying effort.
Fue un esfuerzo masivo de cabildeo.
        (Not "de vestíbulo").

A striking example of modulation can be seen in a key word-play in the epic gaucho poem "Martín Fierro." The situation is this: the gaucho Martín Fierro is at a dance and wants to provoke a fight with another gaucho by insulting his woman. He says to her, in the Spanish original by José Hernández: "Va...ca...yendo gente al baile." To which she replies: "Más vaca será su madre." One translator (Frank Carrino) renders it this way: "Cow...ming to the dance?" and "A bigger cow is your mother." A second translator (Walter Owen) does this: "It's a little bit...chilly tonight." and "The bigger bitch your mother."

There are a number of categories of modulation, which Vázquez-Ayora describes and gives examples of.[55] Sometimes the modulation involves parts of the body used in common expressions: "up to my nose" = "hasta las cejas"; "hand to hand combat" = "combate cuerpo a cuerpo." Or systems of measurement: "he was many miles away" = "estaba a muchos kilómetros" (but be careful if a more precise measurement is involved, in which case 1.6 kilometers equals a mile). Or changes in the symbol used: "within earshot" = "a pocos pasos"; "at a snail's pace" = "a paso de tortuga"; "decision-making" = "toma de decisiones"; "five o'clock shadow" = "sombra de barba"; "fat cats" = "peces gordos."

Application: The ultimate test of whether a translator has modulated correctly is to try it out on a native speaker. The translator him/herself may be too close to the work to be able to make an objective judgement. Read the final version aloud to a native speaker and ask if it sounds natural. If the response is that it does not, or "it sounds like a translation," then the modulation may be faulty. Pay particular attention to any idiomatic or idiosyncratic expressions in the SL which may have been inadvertently translated word for word, instead of modulated into the TL.

D. TRANSLATION PROBLEMS AND TECHNIQUES.

Dictionaries and Glossaries.

If there is one thing the translator needs to understand about dictionaries, it is that **they do not translate.** Bilingual (i.e., Spanish-English and English-Spanish) dictionaries only give word-for-word equivalencies between specific words in the two languages. They do not deal with the contextual meaning of a word, nor do they address the idiomatic or metaphoric meaning (unless they are specialized and extensive dictionaries of idioms and metaphors). Because of this, a dictionary can only "translate" at the word-for-word literal surface level, and cannot reach down to the deep meaning level where the translator needs to work. The possibility of partial false cognates and multiple meanings for a word should alert the translator to the fact that a bilingual dictionary is an unreliable tool.

Put another way, the only person who can use a bilingual dictionary safely is a bilingual person who probably doesn't need to use it in the first place. The irony of this statement raises the interesting question of what a bilingual dictionary is good for. They do have a purpose: dictionaries can serve to jog the memory of a bilingual person and suggest other synonyms which s/he might have forgotten or overlooked. Bilingual dictionaries, if they are extensive, can also tell a translator whether or not there are multiple meanings for the word being looked up. If only one meaning is given, then the translator has some assurance that there is only one meaning for the word in the TL, and thus the possibilities for error are diminished. Bilingual dictionaries can also be used effectively with monolingual dictionaries, as the following suggests.

Example: the problem of translating "nail factory." A careless use of a bilingual dictionary led the translator to use the first equivalent given, which was "uña." Thus, the unfortunate translator rendered "nail factory" as "fábrica de uñas," which is "finger-nail factory." However, had the translator looked up the first word s/he found ("uñas") in a monolingual Spanish dictionary, it would have been clear that there was a problem, since "uñas" would have been defined in Spanish as "parte córnea que cubre la punta de los dedos." Going back to the bilingual dictionary the conscientious translator would then have selected the second meaning, "clavo," and checking in the monolingual Spanish dictionary would have found the definition as "pieza de hierro con cabeza y punta que se hunde en algún cuerpo para asegurar alguna cosa." If the dictionary were an illustrated one, there might also be a picture of a nail, further confirming that this was the correct choice.

The serious translator thus needs good extensive monolingual dictionaries in both SL and TL, as well as a bilingual dictionary. Ideally, the bilingual dictionary would also have a section on idioms and proverbs, as well as an indication of false or partially false cognates and examples of usage. Supplementary dictionaries would provide specialized technical terms, regionalisms and colloquialisms. The translator may also wish to consult an etymological dictionary to see the origin of the word in question, or an historical dictionary to see how the word was used and changed its meaning over time. In Spanish the authoritative dictionary is that of the **Real Academia de la Lengua**, while for English the equivalent is the **Oxford Dictionary of the English Language**. The cost and size of these masterpieces make ownership prohibitive for most translators, but they are generally available in university libraries for consultation. Coramina's *Diccionario Etimológico* is the standard reference work for Spanish word origins and first recorded citations in the literature. The translator working in a scientific or technical field will need to obtain bilingual and monolingual specialized dictionaries. These frequently fall behind current developments in the field, and the translator must stay on top of these developments by personal contact with other translators, membership in professional organizations (including translator's associations), and reading the latest literature in his/her field in both the SL and TL.

Glossaries are word lists which give equivalencies between words in two languages. They are abbreviated dictionaries, and tend to be rather specialized. Being specialized, they can dispense with basic words and concentrate on those which have special meaning for their particular field. A good source of these glossaries are the specialized international organizations (UN, OAS, IDB, IMF, World Bank), large translation bureaus, and other translators. Most translators keep a record of words which have caused them problems in the past. These can be filed on 3x5 index cards, or in computer programs with a sorting function that allows the lists to be modified easily and reorganized alphabetically.

E. COGNATES.

fc = false cognate   pc = partial cognate (be careful)
pfc = partial false cognate (be very careful)

ELEVADOR (pfc) = elevator only in some countries (Mexico).
    A more generally used term is "ascensor."
EMBARAZADA (fc) = to be pregnant.
    ≠ embarrassed; instead use "apenado" or "mortificado."
EMOCIONARSE (pfc) = to be deeply moved or touched.
    ≠ to become emotional in the sense of being excited.
ENTRENAMIENTO (pfc) = training mainly in the military sense.
    Otherwise use: adiestramiento, formación.
ENTRETENER (pfc) = to occupy one's attention or distract.
    ≠ entertain in sense of amusement; instead use "divertir."

ESCOLAR (fc) ≠ scholar; instead use "estudioso" or "erudito"
= schoolboy or schoolgirl.
ESTAMPA (fc) ≠ stamp; instead use "sello" or "estampilla."
= picture, especially a religious one.
EXITO (fc) = success: "la película fue un éxito."
≠ exit in sense of way out; instead use "salida."
EXPERIMENTAR (pfc) = experiment in the sense of trying out.
≠ experiment in the sense of experiencing something;
instead use "sentir."

F. PROVERBS AND IDIOMS.

Echar flores   To flatter.
Echarse un trago   To take a drink.
El hombre propone y Dios dispone.   Man proposes, God disposes.
El que mucho abarca poco aprieta.
    Don't bite off more than you can chew.
El tiempo es oro.   Time is money.
En aquel entonces   At that time.
En boca cerrada no entran moscas.   Silence is golden.
En breve plazo   In a short time.
En calidad de   In the capacity of.
En cuero (also encuerado, encuerada)   Naked; in your birthday suit.

LESSON 11

A. HISTORY OF TRANSLATION.

Translation in Spain's Golden Age.

During the Golden Age of Spanish culture and literature (16th and 17th Centuries) good translation was highly valued as the mechanism by which to gain access to the Latin and Greek classics, as well as the conduit through which the best in Spanish writing could be transmitted to the rest of Europe. At the same time, the respect for Arabic scientific and medical writings (and the need to translate from them) continued, despite the fact that the Moors had been expelled from Spain along with the Jews in the fateful year of 1492. These aspects of Spanish Humanism in the Renaissance did much to shape the Spanish attitude towards literary translation. In this period the English language acquired a number of Spanish words. English lexicographers began to accumulate lists of Spanish words, beginning with John Thorius in 1590, and for the next two centuries this British interest in the Spanish language facilitated translation into the two languages as well as the mutual borrowing of words.[56]

The glory of the old Toledo school of translation had diminished considerably with the expulsion of the Moors and Jews from Spain in 1492, but in many of the old Arab quarters of Spanish cities the tradition of translation from Arabic to Latin or Spanish continued, although frequently in disguise to avoid the suspicions of the Inquisition. The first known Spanish translation of the Muslim Holy Book, the Koran, was made in 1456, but after 1492 the situation of the Arabs left in Spain changed drastically. Those who chose to stay in Spain were known as "Moriscos," and were forced to accept Christian baptism as a condition for their remaining. Any Islamic religious rituals were carried out in secret, and the Holy Writings had to be kept hidden. As the years passed they grew increasingly unable to read the Koran in the original Arabic, and turned more and more to Spanish translations of their Holy Book.

But this in turn violated one of the tenets of the Muslim faith, which required them to read and recite their scripture in Arabic. The solution was to write in Spanish, but in Arabic-looking characters known as "Aljamaido." Even though many of these works were destroyed by the Inquisition, some have survived, and bear witness to the laborious task of translating and then copying the Muslim Holy Book by hand. In the year 1606, a Morisco copier of the Koran in Spain made this marginal notation in a mixture of Castilian, Aljamaido and Arabic:[57]

"Esta eskrito en letra de kristyanos ... rruega y suplica que por estar en dicha letra no lo tengan en menos de lo kes, antes en mucho; porque pues esta asi declarado, esta mas a vista de los muçlimes que saben leer el cristiano y no la letra de los muçlimes. Porque es cierto que dixo el annabî Muhammad *salla Allahu alayhi wa-sallam* que la mejor lengwa era la ke se entendía."

Translation of the passage: "It is written in the letters of the Christians: (the writer) begs that on account of being in those letters it not be belittled, but rather respected; because, being set down in this way, it can better be seen by those Muslims who know how to read Christian, but not Muslim, letters. For it is true that the Prophet Muhammad (peace be unto him) said that the best language was the one that could be understood."

The relationship of Arab and Christian (and the problem of translation) shows up at numerous points in the Spanish masterpiece of this period: the **Don Quijote de la Mancha** of Miguel de Cervantes. Cervantes attributes the authorship of his book to a variety of characters and translators, some Moorish and some Christian, and expresses his opinions on translators in the process. At one particular point[58], Cervantes gives us a metaphor for translation which is frequently cited by contemporary theoreticians and practitioners of translation: "Pero con todo eso, me parece que el traducir de una lengua en otra, como no sea de las reinas de las lenguas, griega y latina, es como quien mira los tapices flamencos por el revés: que aunque se veen las figuras, son llenas de hilos que las escurecen, y no se veen con la lisura y tez de la haz." Cervantes is telling us that (with the exception of Greek and Latin, whose classical beauty cannot be ruined by even a bad translation), the challenge to translators is to keep their finished product from looking like the reverse side of a Flemish tapestry, with its negative images and loose threads.

B. TRANSLATION TIDBIT.
A Mexican came across the border at El Paso, Texas to buy some socks. Unfortunately he spoke no English and the clerk no Spanish, so the clerk started pulling items off the shelf hoping to find the one thing the Mexican wanted. Finally he showed the Mexican a pair of socks. The delighted Mexican responded by saying "Eso sí que es," which caused the American clerk to reply, "How come you can't speak English but you can spell it?"[59]

C. THEORY OF TRANSLATION.

Transposition.

Transposition is the second key translation technique derived from linguistics, specifically a theoretical branch of syntactical analysis (grammar) known as "generative or transformational grammar." Transposition is based on the idea that a given thought can be expressed in a number of different ways without doing undue violence to the deep structure concept involved. Some of these transposed forms will sound more natural than others in the target language, while some will not be possible for grammatical or stylistic reasons. The skilled translator must be able to generate a range of these transpositions (sometimes unconsciously) and select the one that sounds most natural and even elegant in the target language. Example:

He presented an excellent draft of the treaty.
Presentó un excelente borrador del tratado.
El presentó un excelente borrador del tratado.
El borrador del tratado que presentó fue excelente.
Excelente fue el borrador del tratado que presentó.
El tratado en borrador que presentó fue excelente.
Lo que presentó (el borrador del tratado) fue excelente.
El borrador del tratado que fue presentado fue excelente.
El borrador del tratado que se presentó fue excelente.
Lo excelente fue el borrador del tratado que se presentó. (etc.)

Transposition is usually easier to do when going from English to Spanish because Spanish allows greater freedom of word order. However, it is also possible to transpose when going from Spanish to English:

Que lástima que Jorge es tan estúpido.
What a shame that Jorge is so stupid.
What a shame that Jorge acts so stupidly.
Stupid Jorge - what a shame.
What a shame that Jorge is capable of such stupidity.
Jorge is so stupid, and that is a shame.

In these examples we have not changed the basic deep meaning, although the word order and function of several of the words have changed. "Stupid," for example, is variously a noun, an adjective, and an adverb.

Transposition can be "tight," in the sense that the same words are used and only their function or order is changed, or "loose" if synonyms are brought in. In such a case the possibilities are almost endless, and the translator is faced with some hard decisions involving nuances of meaning. In the first example we could use the word "acuerdo" instead of tratado, and "versión inicial" instead of "borrador." The permutations soon become astronomical. And yet the translator must run these through his or her mind, seeking the one that best captures the deep meaning and that sounds most natural in the target language. As was the case with modulation, Vázquez-Ayora lists a wide range of transposition possibilities[60], including adverb for verb; adverb for noun; adverb for adjective; past participle for noun; verb for adjective; adjective for noun; possessive for definite article, etc. It is also possible to combine transposition and modulation in a single process, so that the end product produces a very large number of possibilities from which the translator must select one. Because of the quantity of permutations that are possible, working translators obviously do not write out all of them. But they may jot down a couple of the better ones and mull them over before making the choice. As was the case with modulation, the translator may find after a while that he/she is too close to the mechanics of the process to make a wise final choice. At this point one can once again call on the friendly native speaker to pick the one that sounds "most natural."

Application: As an exercise, it would be worthwhile for beginning translators to go through the process of generating as many transpositions as possible. With time, the process should become automatic, at least to the extent that only a small number of transpositions are tentatively selected before making the final choice.

D. TRANSLATION PROBLEMS AND TECHNIQUES.

Academic and Medical Translation.

    Although it might seem that these two categories of translation are relatively simple and straightforward, they illustrate the relationship between language and culture, and the traps that uncertain knowledge of a subject can pose for translators.

Academic Translations. The general problem in the translation of academic terms, transcripts and credentials is that the terms used are not always equivalent, even if they might have cognates in both languages. The Spanish term "colegio" is usually not a "college" (i.e., university-level institute), but a secondary school (frequently a private one), and the term can be translated as "school" or "secondary school." The degree awarded by that "colegio" is usually the "bachillerato," which is the equivalent of a U.S. high school diploma, and not the U.S. baccalaureate (university) degree. Although the term "maestría" exists in many Latin American educational systems, it may or may not be equivalent to the U.S. "master's" degree usually requiring one to two years of full-time study after the B.A. The Latin American "licenciatura" is sometimes used as the equivalent of the M.A. because it generally represents five years of university study, but there are many variations in subject matter and level of study. The term "curso" has a wide variety of meanings which can include the exact English cognate of a single university "course" of perhaps three credit hour value. But "curso" can also mean a related sequence of courses, an academic year, or a complete course of studies equivalent to a major.

In translating a grade transcript the course titles generally are straightforward, but the grading systems used in the U.S., Latin America and Spain show much variation. The system most commonly in use in Latin America is a 10 or 100 point one, with adjectival ratings sometimes coupled to certain grade levels. The term "sobresaliente" is equivalent to "outstanding" or "excellent" (especially when "excellent" = A in the U.S. system). "Notable" is usually equivalent to "very good." The translator may notice that failing grades are infrequent in transcripts from Latin America. This is because the educational system often permits a series of exams and re-exams to validate a subject one has failed. It should be noted that the U.S. letter grade system is very confusing when translated into Spanish, and if this needs to be done the translator may have to explain the relationship between the letter grade and the "quality point" equivalent, so that it is clear that an "A" means a maximum of 4.0 out of 4.0; that a "B" means 3.0 out of 4.0, etc. But even here mathematical equivalencies are deceptive, since a "D" is technically a passing grade, but represents only 1.0 out of 4.0, and is not the same as 25% (i.e., 1.0/4.0).

Medical Translations. As Simon and Gonzalez-Lee have pointed out,[61] medical translation and interpretation might seem simple, but they also have a number of difficulties. The apparent simplicity stems from the fact that much medical terminology has Latin and Greek roots, and thus has valid cognates in many languages, including Spanish and English. Many medical terms dealing with anatomy, diseases, medication and treatment fit into this category. However, many terms do not, and the translator should be cautious about false cognates.

A problem which medical T/I shares with legal T/I is that of register: the translator/interpreter is an intermediary between a professional (doctor, lawyer) who speaks the language and jargon at a high register, while the patients or clients may come from a wide range of backgrounds with a wide variety of language registers. This difficulty is especially apparent when interpreting.

An added complication is the widespread influence of folk medicine, with its own terminology which is not generally understood or recognized by the medical profession. The patient may have a vocabulary for his/her symptoms which is incomprehensible to the professional medical practitioner even if there were no language barrier. Parts of the body and types of sensations may have a folk description which is colorful, idiosyncratic, and deeply rooted in folk medicine and popular beliefs. At the same time the formally-schooled health professional's language and approaches may seem of doubtful relevance to the patient and his/her family. Faced with such situations the translator/interpreter must be a cultural bridge as well as a linguistic one.

E. COGNATES.
fc = false cognate   pc = partial cognate (be careful)
pfc = partial false cognate (be very careful)

FABRICA (fc) ≠ cloth fabric; instead use "tela."
    = factory or plant.
FACULTAD (pfc) = school in a university: "Facultad de Derecho;"
    also can mean a physical or mental faculty.
    ≠ the faculty of a university; instead use "profesorado."
FASTIDIOSO (fc) ≠ fastidious; instead use "meticuloso."
    = boring or irritating.
FEUDO (pfc) ≠ feud in sense of fight or hate; instead use "odio."
    = fief in a medieval sense.
FIRMA (fc) = signature.
    ≠ firm in sense of company;
    instead use "empresa," "compañía."
FISCAL (pfc) = fiscal (adjective) in sense of "fiscal year."
    But it can also mean "governmental" in a general sense.
    The verb "fiscalizar" usually means to officially check,
    supervise or investigate.
FISICO (pfc) = physicist.
    ≠ physician; instead use "médico."
FORMA (pfc) = form in sense of shape.
    ≠ form in sense of a form to be filled out;
    instead use "formulario" or "planilla."

F. PROVERBS AND IDIOMS.

En efectivo   In cash.
En el peligro se conoce el amigo.
       A friend in need is a friend indeed.
En fin   In short; oh well.
En hora buena   Luckily, safely. Also: congratulations.
En mangas de camisa   In shirt sleeves.
En punto   On the dot (on time).
En su apogeo   At one's peak.
En un abrir y cerrar de ojos   In the twinkling of an eye.
En un descuido   When least expected; taken by surprise.
Encargarse de   To take charge of.

Figure 11-1. Translation in Mexico, 16th Century.
The Spanish priest Bernardino de Sahagún is on the left.

LESSON 12

A. HISTORY OF TRANSLATION.

Translation and the "Black Legend" of Spain.

Translation (or more accurately, mistranslation) was a weapon used in creating the "Black Legend" against Spain, and to a lesser extent, Portugal. The Black Legend was an attempt by polemicists in England, Holland and France to portray the Spanish in the New World as cruel, fanatical, exploitative, and wrong in their policies. The purpose was to diminish the achievements of the Iberians in America and justify the Northern Europeans in their quest to take the Spanish possessions, or the riches they generated, away from them. It was a massive propaganda effort sustained over a period of many years, and which continues to have impact in certain prejudicial attitudes against Hispanics today. To be certain, the Spanish did not act out of exclusively altruistic motives, and many of the charges leveled against them were justified. But the Northern Europeans were consistently emphasizing and distorting the negative aspects of the Spanish and Portuguese conquest and colonial regimes, while presenting their own actions in the best possible light.

The role of translation in this process involved taking the Spanish accounts of their activities in the New World and selectively distorting portions of them. When, for example, the Spanish priest Bartolomé de las Casas attempted to defend the Indians from the abuses of the Spanish administrators in America, his writings were distorted and mistranslated by the English and others to provide documentation for the Black Legend. Las Casas came to America in 1502, and after a stint of exploiting Indians himself in the mines and lands he owned, he developed a conscience about the exploitation of the Indians, entered the priesthood, and became a life-long crusader against these wrongs. In 1547 he wrote his most powerful tract, the "Brevísima Relación de la Destrucción de las Indias," in which he presented in gruesome detail the excesses of the Spaniards. Although he exaggerated, his accusations were justified, and they did cause the

Spanish Crown to institute reforms. However, his tract also reached the Northern Europeans, who seized upon it as proof of the Black Legend's truth. In a short period of time the work was translated into Latin, English, French, German and Dutch. Here is the subtitle carried in the English translation of 1606: "Popery truly Display'd in its Bloody Colours: Or a Faithful Narrative of the Horrid and Unexampled Massacres, Butcheries, and all manner of Cruelties, that Hell and Malice could invent, committed by the Popish Spanish Party on the Inhabitants of West-India... Composed first in Spanish by Bartholomew de las Casas, a Bishop there, and an Eye-Witness of most of these Barbarous Cruelties; afterwards translated by him into Latin, then by other hands into ... Modern English."[62]

An example of more subtle but still deliberate mis-translation into English in order to serve the Black Legend was Pedro Cieza de Leon's *Crónica del Perú*, published in 1553. Cieza de Leon was an impartial and respected chronicler whose work does not have the polemic quality of that of Bartolomé de las Casas. Indeed, his book provides the historian with very detailed accounts of the Incas at the time of the conquest. The book was first translated into English by John Stevens in 1709, and again by Clements Markham in the 19th Century. This latter translation, in particular, has been strongly criticized for its distortions which support the Black Legend.[63] There are extensive omissions and mistranslations that are not obvious to the reader unless a close comparison with the original is made. Markham consistently omitted passages that portrayed the Indians in a bad light, such as those describing their sexual perversions and their cannibalistic practices. In another he takes an incident when Indians commit suicide and changes it so as to make their deaths appear to be the result of their wanton killing by the Spaniards.

B. TRANSLATION TIDBIT.

The origin of the word "gringo" is unknown. One version has it that it comes from the song "Green Grow the Rushes" which was sung by U.S. troops in the 1846-1848 war with Mexico. However, the word was in use before then. Sarmiento, for example, calls Sir Walter Scott a "gringo." The word may be a corruption of "griego," in the sense that "it's Greek to me."[64]

C. THEORY OF TRANSLATION.

Addition.

If the content of the TL translation is not the same as that of the SL original, then we may have either addition or omission (loss) between the two versions. We can diagram this as follows:

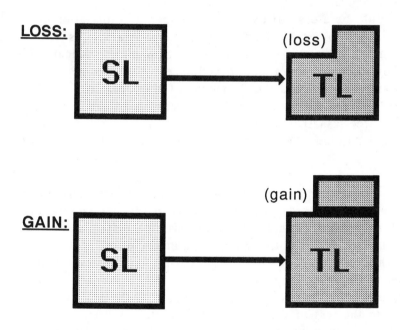

Figure 12-1: Loss and Gain in Translation

Because of the characteristics of the two languages (as discussed above in Lesson 9 on comparative linguistics), omission of specific words is more common going from Spanish to English, especially with grammatical forms such as articles and possessives, which are used less in English. Conversely, addition is more common in going from English to Spanish, because of the need to expand or explain very concise English phrases which have a heavy density of adjectives and nouns. Additions (and omissions) can be inadvertent, or they can be unavoidable due to syntactic, semantic or lexical reasons. An examples of a syntactic addition when going into English would be the need to expand the Spanish possessive "su" in order to avoid ambiguities.[65]

Semantic additions can occur when something in the SL is not included because it would be obvious to most readers of that language, but should be included in the TL because of the probability that the typical TL reader would not be aware of that information. This would be a case of explicitly laying out information in the TL which was implicit in the SL. A frequent example is the implicit information associated with common place names, political positions, etc. For example, an Argentine audience would not need to be told that Raul Alfonsín was the President of their nation, but if a story about President Alfonsín were being translated from a Buenos Aires news source to a U.S. one, it would be wise to add the information that Raul Alfonsín had been President of that nation from 1985 to 1989.

Lexical mismatches can also lead to additions. For example, if we translate the word "girlfriend" into Spanish as "novia" we have added the possibility that the young lady in question might be either a "girlfriend" in the dating sense, a fiancée, or a "bride," since the Spanish word can have all of these meanings. The lexical mismatch between the two languages has forced us to add a piece of information that makes the TL different from the SL. If the point is central to the rest of the piece being translated, it may be necessary to add words to make the meaning absolutely unambiguous.

D. TRANSLATION PROBLEMS AND TECHNIQUES.

<u>Legal Translation.</u>

A number of texts and other reference materials have been written for the legal field, especially as it relates to court translation and interpretation in the U.S.[66] The numerous international organizations (UN, OAS, World Bank, IDB, IMF) have produced a large number of glossaries and other translation aids which should also be consulted.[67] The typical translator can expect to be asked to translate a number of legal documents in his/her career. These would include such items as birth and marriage certificates, contracts, court decisions, family documents, etc. The translator must approach these with care and an understanding of the legal system from which the documents came, and the intended use which the requestor will make of them. Frequently the translator may be working across two legal systems: the "case law" Anglo-Saxon system prevalent in the United States, and the "code law" Napoleonic system of Latin America.

To illustrate the problems inherent in dealing with two legal systems, Englebert cites the problem of the concept of "notary" in the U.S. and the apparent cognate "notario" in the Latin American legal system.[68] In the United States a "notary" is usually a legal clerk, administrative assistant or junior bank official who is registered with the local legal system for the purpose of administering oaths, authenticating signatures and certifying other documents. He/she performs the role of notary usually as a supplementary activity to his/her primary employment in a law firm, bank or other office, charging a nominal fee to "notarize" documents and signatures and administer oaths. In Latin America, however, the "notario" is usually a lawyer with extensive legal training who drafts legal documents, advises clients, and keeps a registry of documents which s/he has prepared or legalized. The powers, authority and responsibilities of a "notario" are thus much greater than those of a "notary." This difference led to a situation in California and other border states where irresponsible U.S. notaries were preying on Hispanic Americans by suggesting that they were able to perform certain functions for a fee in the U.S. legal system similar to the role of "notarios públicos" in Latin America.[69]

E. COGNATES.

fc = false cognate   pc = partial cognate (be careful)
pfc = partial false cognate (be very careful)

FORMAL (pfc) = reliable, trustworthy.
       ≠ ceremonious or formal dress;
       instead use "ceremonioso" and "de etiqueta."

GABINETE (pfc) = cabinet only for a body of ministers or advisors.
≠ cabinet as a piece of furniture; instead use "vitrina."
GENTILMENTE (fc) ≠ gently;
instead use "suavemente" or "cuidadosamente."
= charmingly, kindly.
GRACIA (pfc) = grace, but also means "joke," "funny":
"Juan es muy gracioso."
GRANADA (pfc) = explosive projectile and the country "Grenada."
But also = pomegranate as the fruit.
GRATIFICAR (pfc) = to tip or compensate.
≠ gratify; instead use "dar satisfacción" or "dar placer."
GROSERIA (fc) ≠ grocery store; instead use "tienda."
= coarse, boorish or crude act.
HARMONIZAR (pfc) = create harmony.
Also = coordinate, bring into phase or synchronize.

F. PROVERBS AND IDIOMS.
Entrar en materia   To get down to business; to get to the point.
Entre bastidores   Behind the scenes.
Entre la espada y la pared   Between a rock and a hard place.
Es harina de otro costal   A horse of a different color.
Esforzarse por   To strive for.
Este arroz ya se coció.   It's in the bag.
Estar a punto de   To be about to.
Estar chiflado   To be nuts.
Estar de acuerdo   To be in agreement with.
Estar de luto   To be in mourning.

LESSON 13

A. HISTORY OF TRANSLATION.

Translation in the 17th and 18th Centuries.

The major advances in the theory and practice of translation in these centuries belong to England, as amply documented by scholars such as Stiner in his *English Translation Theory, 1650-1800*. Not only were there some very important translations being accomplished by British writers, but perhaps more importantly they concerned themselves with how quality translations could be produced, and what the duties of the translator were to both the original writer as well as to the reader of the translation. Because of the practical nature of many of the observations made by British translators of this period, they are still valuable for us today.[70]

By the 17th Century the impact of the Reformation and Counter-reformation and a more powerful Parliament in England had run its course, with the important side effects of invigorating British letters and rekindling interest in the classics, and therefore translation. The status of translators was elevated, to the point that the best translators were given a position of quasi-equality to the original writers they were rendering into English. The most prominent figure in this field in the 17th Century was John Dryden, who not only was a major translator, but also an individual who established a basic typology, or classification, of translations: they could either be "metaphrase" (word for word), "paraphrase" (more sense for sense), or "imitation" (in which the translator assumes considerable liberties with both the word and sense of the original). Dryden also acknowledged the basic dilemma of the translator caught between being faithful to the original and yet also intelligible, when he said: "It is impossible to translate verbally and well at the same time. 'Tis much like dancing on ropes with fetter'd legs! A man may shun a fall by using caution, but the gracefulness of motion is not to be expected."[71]

Dryden saw translation in very modern terms as a careful balance between the features which make translation an art, a craft, or a science. His detailed rules establish prerequisites for a translator, whom he felt must be master of both the language of the original and his own. As he translates, he must:
- Understand the characteristics that make the author individual.
- Conform his genius as translator to that of the original.
- Be literal when gracefulness can be maintained.
- Make the original author appear as "charming" as possible without violating his true character.
- Make the original author speak contemporary English.
- Not try to improve the original.
- Not try to follow the original so closely that the spirit is lost.

The 18th Century brought a new and useful metaphor for translation: the translator would be like a portrait painter, who would use his own materials to present an accurate portrait of reality which captured the "spirit" of the original, but not necessarily the exact features. Because the translator cannot recreate nature, he must necessarily use a different palette and different colors. But nevertheless his guiding principle should be to catch the spirit and strive for the same impact. In this task he had equal responsibilities to the original writer, to the reader, and to his own standards.

Late in the 18th Century Alexander Fraser Tytler, Lord Woodhouselee (1747-1814), produced a classic work in the field of translation, his 1792 *Essay on the Principles of Translation*. Here he established simple basic principles and illustrated them exhaustively with examples from a wide range of languages. His three fundamental principles of translation were:[72]

1. A translation should give a complete transcript of the ideas of the original work.

2. The style and manner of writing should be of the same character as that of the original.

3. A translation should have all the ease of the original composition.

B. TRANSLATION TIDBIT.

In Panama a few years ago, you could get into serious trouble with the military by mentioning two fruits: "piña" or "mango." "Piña" was a reference to the nickname "cara de piña," which in turn is a commentary on General Manuel A. Noriega's acne problem. "Mango" was short for "Manuel A. Noriega go."[73]

Susana Greiss tells this true story from her experience.[74] She was interpreting in a trial involving a workman who had injured himself in a fall from a scaffolding. The man was being cross-examined as follows:

"¿Usted estaba armando el andamio?" "Sí"
"¿Cuántos hombres estaban haciéndolo?" "Unicamente yo y Luis"
At this point the opposing lawyer jumped up and demanded:
"Yeah? So who was this guy Armando you were just talking about?"

C. THEORY OF TRANSLATION.

Omission.

Omissions in translations, like additions, can also be inadvertent or forced by syntactic, semantic, or lexical reasons. The semantic example given in the previous lesson would also work in reverse: if a news story about President Alfonsin's visit to the United States were written in English for a U.S. audience it would describe his position, politics, tenure, etc. This material might very well be omitted if the story in English SL was being translated into Spanish for an Argentine TL audience.

The flowery and redundant nature of many stock Spanish phrases, especially when prescribed formulas are involved in situations such as speeches and business letters, requires omissions when going into English. One can imagine the effect that the following sentence in a business letter would have on a U.S. executive: "Without any other motive, I take this welcome opportunity to express to you my highest consideration and regards, and place myself at your distinguished service for any other matter which you deem convenient."

Both languages (English and Spanish) have their own "filler" words which add nothing to the content of the message and can (and should) be omitted in translation. English sometimes pairs sets of words which are essentially synonyms and are thus redundant. (These are the so-called "doublets," such as bold and courageous, strangers and foreigners, dirt and grime, etc). Some of these represent a fossilized characteristic dating from the time when English was subjected to two cultural tendencies (Anglo and Saxon) when words with roots from both cultures were frequently used. English also sometimes does this with pairs of Latin and Anglo-Saxon words. A Spanish translation could efficiently reduce this to one word without losing the meaning.

In other cases prepositions or other individual words have an idiomatic meaning which should not be translated and can thus be legitimately omitted. In the following phrases the English prepositional phrases in italics function in this matter and are eliminated:
"She is **on her way** down" = "Ella está bajando"
"speed **it up**" = "rápido."

Application: As was the case with addition, the translator needs to be aware of the possibilities and sometimes the requirement to add or omit to keep the translation accurate and idiomatic in the TL.

D. TRANSLATION PROBLEMS AND TECHNIQUES.

Diplomatic Translation.

In diplomacy the shift away from using a single language (French) in recent decades has created a series of problems as well as an increasing demand for qualified translators and interpreters. When French was the language of diplomacy it was the authoritative medium for international treaties, agreements and contracts. Any problems that arose stemmed from relatively infrequent ambiguities within one language. French is a fairly clear and direct language, which led a diplomat to once remark that "it is impossible to lie in

French." However, the use of various languages in diplomacy for political and nationalistic reasons has led to the problem of deciding which text in which language is the authoritative one. Sometimes this is defined in the treaty itself, and sometimes it is understood that the nation hosting a conference or acting as repository of a treaty will also provide the authoritative text. Another approach is that if there is a difficulty caused by ambiguity it should penalize the party responsible for drafting that part which created the problem.

Unfortunately, in the field of diplomacy the spectacular errors and gaffes of translators/interpreters frequently make the news rather than their routine daily accomplishments. In 1977 a part-time contract interpreter for the Department of State traveling with President Jimmy Carter to Poland committed a series of embarrassing errors. At his airport arrival he rendered Carter's comment on leaving the U.S. as "abandoning" the U.S. (the same error would have been likely in Spanish, where "abandonar" frequently means departing, not "leaving to its own devices"). More spectacularly, when Carter spoke of the Polish people's "desires" for the future, it came out as "lusts."

Historically the United States Foreign Service has suffered from a lack of qualified translators/interpreters. Frequently the function is performed by exiles with an axe to grind, who have a special and sometimes difficult political relationship with their country of origin. For example, when Kissinger and Nixon traveled to China in the 1970's much of the translation in preparation for their visit was done by Chinese from Taiwan, whose vocabulary and construction were obvious to the President's hosts in the People's Republic of China.[75]

National leaders will frequently blame translators/ interpreters for "mistakes" when in fact they are using this as an excuse for their own oratorical excesses or slips of the tongue. The officially translated written texts of volatile speakers such as Libya's Moammar Gadhafi's frequently are softer and more reasonable than their extemporaneous remarks on the air. In a recent example, Gadhafi spoke of "abolishing the nonaligned movement completely," but the transcript which followed referred to his wish to "surpass" the movement, thus avoiding the more aggressive phrasing of the words he spoke on the air.[76]

In the U.S. a recent example was the CIA's manual for the "Contra" guerrillas fighting the Sandinista government of Nicaragua. The version picked up by journalists in the field spoke of the need to "neutralizar" Sandinista officials, and to employ "uso selectivo de la violencia." When taken to task by members of Congress for inciting unwarranted violence and even assassination, the CIA argued that the Spanish word "neutralizar" did not mean the same thing as the English "neutralize," which in intelligence jargon means "kill." Nor, they argued, did "uso selectivo de la violencia" mean "selective use of violence." Translators in the Congressional Research Service disagreed, arguing that the cognates were valid, and that the CIA was indeed telling the Contras to use violence and assassination in violation of presidential orders.[77]

E. COGNATES.
fc = false cognate   pc = partial cognate (be careful)
pfc = partial false cognate (be very careful)

HONESTO (fc) ≠ honest; instead use "honrado."
    = decent, decorous, modest.
HUMANO (pfc) = human in sense of human being.
    Also = humane in the sense of compassionate.
IGNORAR (fc) = to be unaware: "ignoro lo que pasó con Juan."
    ≠ to deliberately not pay attention to;
    instead use "no prestar atención" or "no hacer caso."
ILUSTRADO (pfc) = to have illustrations in the sense of pictures.
    Also = learned or enlightened:
    "el profesor es un hombre ilustrado."
IMPONERSE (pfc) = to assert oneself, to be authoritative.
    ≠ bother or cause a problem; instead use "molestar."
IMPRESIONANTE (pfc) = usually stronger than the English
    "impressive"; generally means: shocking, startling, alarming.
INEDITO (pfc) = unpublished.
    Also = unheard of, novel, innovative, unprecedented.

INQUIETUD (pfc) = uneasiness.
Also usually means intellectual curiosity or doubt.
INTEGRAL (pfc) = integral in the mathematical sense.
Also = comprehensive: "el concepto de la defensa integral."
INTERVENIR (pfc) = interfere.
Also = operate surgically.

F. PROVERBS AND IDIOMS.

Estar de moda To be fashionable.
Estar en el pellejo de otro To be in someone else's shoes.
Estar en las nubes To be in the clouds; daydreaming.
Estar en vigor To be in effect (as in a treaty).
Estar en vísperas de On the eve of.
Estar muy metido en To be deeply involved in.
Estar para To be about to.
Estar quebrado To be broke, bankrupt.
Fiesta quinceañera Coming-out party for a young woman (age 15).
Formar parte de To be a part of.

Figure 13-1. Fray Bartolomé de las Casas.

LESSON 14

A. HISTORY OF TRANSLATION.

Romanticism and 19th Century translation.

The spirit of 19th Century Romanticism (especially in Latin America) rejected the cold and rigid laws of Neoclassicism and freed the human spirit so that it could soar to greater heights of emotion and unbridled creativity. However, Romanticism treated translators in two rather contradictory manners. One was to simply see translation as a way of permitting access to unbridled spirits and emotions in other languages; the translator's job was not to create, but to allow the romantic spirit to flow faithfully from one language to the other. The other Romantic treatment of translators was to treat them as fellow Romantics and allow **them** the freedom to feel and create as equals in the process. Ideally, this treatment of the translator as a creative genius in his or her own right, who was in touch with the feelings of the original writer, would then result in a great enriching of the language and literature of the target language.[78]

As might be expected, the Romantics were much concerned with the translation of poetry, and a great deal of the attention paid to translation in this period dealt with the issue of whether or not poetry could be adequately translated (or at all). The poet Percy Bysshe Shelley was adamant that translation could not do poetry justice unless one could go back to the original "seed" of thought in the poet's mind:

"It were as wise to cast a violet into a crucible that you might discover the formal principle of its colour and odour, as to seek to transfuse from one language to another the creations of a poet. The plant must spring again from its seed, or it will bear no flower - and this is the burthen of the curse of Babel."[79]

On the other hand, some of the best poetry translations ever accomplished into the English language were carried out in this period - by poets. Matthew Arnold argued that the purpose of translation (especially of poetry) should be to achieve the same effect on a reader that the original would have on those who could read it in the language of the writer. Thus, accuracy must be sacrificed for the aesthetic and emotional effect. The Romantic poet who best illustrates this principle was Edward FitzGerald (1809-1883), whose translation from the Persian of the *Rubaiyat* of Omar Khayyam carries deep impact in the English.

This period in the history of translation includes the time when the United States as a new nation on the world scene was beginning to consider the need for translation/interpretation in the conduct of its diplomacy and trade in the world. The State Department established the "Department of Foreign Affairs" in 1781 with one French interpreter and one French translator. A Spanish translator was added five years later. A few years later the staff was expanded to ten, but clearly this was not adequate, since substantial amounts of translation work had to be contracted out.[80]

B. TRANSLATION TIDBIT.
Gregory Rabassa's comments on translation and translators: a translator "is a writer, but one whose elbows are lashed to the arms of the chair, as it were."
"A closer analogy might be one between translation and those numbered canvases we have now, where the painter follows instructions as to which color goes where, with the result a reproduction of some existing painting."[81]

C. THEORY OF TRANSLATION.

Lexical Problems and Semantic Mapping.

As noted in previous lessons, the translator frequently has problems with words which seem to be equivalent from SL to TL, but whose range of possible meaning is different from one language to the other. One example used previously was girlfriend and novia, and the problem is that although "novia" can mean girlfriend, it can also mean fiancée and bride, which the English word girlfriend does not.

For the novice translator this problem poses many traps. One of them occurs when a bilingual dictionary is used to try and find equivalent words from SL to TL. Bilingual dictionaries simply list word equivalencies, without defining ranges of meaning and areas of overlap with other meanings. To compensate for this deficiency it is possible to then consult single-language dictionaries to pin down the range of meaning, and a really dedicated translator will consult single-language etymological and expanded dictionaries to find the history of the word usage and place it in specific contexts. But relatively few translators do this, with sometimes unfortunate results.

False cognates frequently involve problems with lexical mismatches. These sometimes develop because the words evolved differently in each language from a single etymological root, or perhaps because the similarity is only coincidental and there is no linkage at all between the words. In any case, false cognates are the bane of the translator, and one of the quickest ways to test the translation competency of an individual is to subject him or her to a text which is loaded with the traps of false cognates.

In order to avoid this problem we can use a helpful device which is derived from linguistic theory: semantic mapping.[82] As the name suggests, semantic mapping means drawing a diagram of the range of meaning of one or more words in ways that will help us avoid traps of the kind mentioned above. The simplest form of semantic mapping is within one language to show how a word can include several others within its meaning. Figure 14-1 illustrates the inclusion of a specific dog (Evita) within the word beagle, which in turn is within the word dog, which is in the word canine. Figure 4-2 shows how these words have one-for-one correspondence (full overlap) with Spanish words (English shown in solid lines, Spanish in dotted).

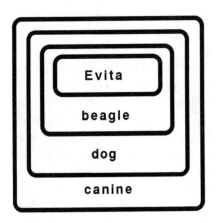

Figure 14-1: Map of words included within others

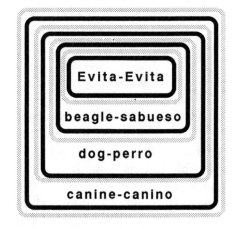

Figure 14-2: One-for-one semantic correspondence
(English = solid lines
Spanish = dotted lines)

On the other hand, the partial overlap situations of novia-girlfriend and nail-uña are shown as follows in Figure 14-3:

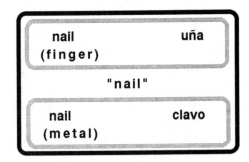

Figure 14-3: Partial semantic overlap
(English = solid lines; Spanish = dotted lines)

These can also be shown in a chain-like presentation (Figure 14-4):

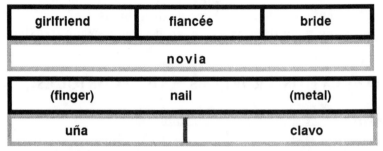

Figure 14-4: Partial semantic overlap

Semantic maps can also be drawn to show juxtaposed meanings, such as the words "union, alliance, coalition, league," all of which share a core concept of joining together, but each of which has a partial domain separate from the central core (Figure 14-5).

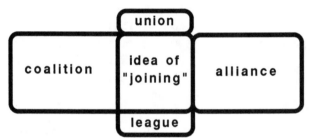

Figure 14-5: Juxtaposed meanings.

We can also diagram polar, or opposite meanings, such as hot/cold, short/tall, night/day (Figure 14-6):

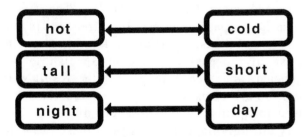

Figure 14-6: Polar (opposite) meanings

Application: Semantic mapping helps us understand relationships between words within one language or across languages. Such mapping can be used as a teaching device, or as a reminder of the pitfalls of using the wrong part of a word's range when translating.

D. TRANSLATION PROBLEMS AND TECHNIQUES.

The Passive Voice and Other Verb Problems.

Because of its Latin roots, the verb structure of Spanish is quite different from English. The student of intermediate and advanced Spanish learns many of these differences, and even the elementary student has to struggle with basic complications such as "ser" and "estar."

Some of the other verb problems which the advanced student of Spanish should be familiar with include:

ENGLISH	SPANISH
one simple past tense	two: preterite and imperfect
subjunctive (rare)	subjunctive (common; many nuances)
"to know"	"saber/conocer"
"do/make"	"hacer"

Many verbs which are not reflexive in English are reflexive in Spanish (ex: wash, fall down, get up, shave, etc). The English modal auxiliaries (will/shall; would/should; may/might; can/could; must) also complicate matters. In this section we will discuss three verb forms which cause the Spanish-English translator problems because, while their use is not incorrect, their appearance seems odd, or "foreign" if used more than occasionally. The first and most common problem is the passive voice. It is frequent in English, but relatively unused in Spanish. As a result, the translator should question any use of the passive voice in Spanish to see if it is required or justified, and then perhaps test the result with a native speaker to see if the use of passive sounds excessive. The passive is legitimately used in Spanish when the agent of the verb's action is specified or very strongly implied, such as in these examples: "The car was stolen by Juan."   "El auto fue robado por Juan."

"The car was stolen today (by the thief)."
"El auto fue robado hoy (por el ladrón)."
In other cases where the agent of the verb's action is not expressed
or stressed, Spanish more naturally would use a direct active voice
or the construction with the reflexive pronoun:
"The house was painted last year"
"Pintaron la casa el año pasado"; "Se pintó la casa el año pasado"
The reflexive construction is especially prevalent in signs:
"Eating is not permitted in the Library"
      Poor: "No está permitido comer en la Biblioteca"
      Better: "No se permite comer en la Biblioteca"
      Best: "Se prohibe comer en la Biblioteca."

A second verb problem is the English present participle (the
gerund: English "-ing" = Spanish "-ando"). As with the passive,
English tends to use it more often, and the translator should ask the
same questions about whether the gerund is permissible or advisable
in Spanish. English tends to use it in progressive tenses more
frequently than Spanish, but Spanish avoids using it when we de-
emphasize how long the action will take:
"What are you eating?"   Possible: "¿Qué estás comiendo?"
                        Better: "¿Qué comes?
English frequently uses the gerund as an adjective; Spanish cannot:
    "decision-making"   "toma de decisiones"
    "interesting idea"   "idea interesante."
Or in place of the Spanish infinitive:
    "Le gusta comer"   "He likes eating"
    "Amar es vivir"   "Loving is living."

Finally, we have the so-called "dramatic present," when the
present tense is used to describe an action in the past to give a more
dramatic impact. It is often used in Spanish but rarely in English:
"San Martín nace en Yapeyú, pero muy joven se traslada a España
para iniciarse en la carrera militar." The English dramatic present
sounds strange: "San Martín is born in Yapeyú, but at an early age he
moves to Spain to start his military career." A more natural-sounding
English translation would use the past tense: "San Martín was born
in Yapeyú, but at an early age he moved to Spain to start his military
career."

E. COGNATES.

fc = false cognate   pc = partial cognate (be careful)
pfc = partial false cognate (be very careful)

INTOXICADO (pfc) = intoxicated generally, but usually means a
     medical or physical reaction to a poison or bad food.
     For intoxicated in the alcoholic or drug sense,
     instead use "ebrio", "borracho" or "drogado."
INTRODUCIR (fc) = to present or insert an idea or object.
     ≠ to present a person to another; instead use "presentar":
     "te presento a José."
INVERTIR (pfc) = to turn upside down.
     Also = to invest money or capital.
JORNADA (fc) ≠ journey; instead use "viaje."
     = day's work; short seminar or workshop.
LABOR (pfc) = has a broader meaning than English "labor,"
     which usually means manual, physical or factory work.
     The Spanish "labor" can also mean mental or
     intellectual work. In the terminology of economics and
     government, English "labor" is translated as "trabajo":
     Ministerio de Trabajo.
LECTURA (fc) = reading.
     ≠ lecture; instead use "conferencia," "ponencia."
LOCAL (pfc) = local in the sense of being close by.
     Also = store premise: "el local 12 del mismo edificio."
LOCALIZAR (pfc) = to make local.
     ≠ locate or find; instead use "situar" or "ubicar."

F. PROVERBS AND IDIOMS.

Fuera de sí   Out of sorts, unconscious.
Fuerte como un roble   As strong as an ox.
Fulano de Tal   So-and-so; John Doe.
Función corrida   All-day program; repeated showings (of a movie).
Ganarse la vida   To earn a living.
Hacer alarde de   To brag, boast.
Hacer escala en   To make a stop at.
Hacer hincapié en   To emphasize, insist on.
Hacer la vista gorda   To wink at; to pretend not to see.

LESSON 15

A. HISTORY OF TRANSLATION.

A late 19th Century translator: José Martí.

José Martí (1853-1895) is usually honored as the great poet, patriot and martyr of Cuban Independence, but he was also a translator of some note. Although he translated literary material for the sheer joy of it, much of the translating he did was imposed on him by economic necessity during his many years of exile in the United States[83]. Martí learned English at an early age, and had begun to translate at thirteen. He continued translating for the rest of his life, including his time as a student in Spain, although the period of his greatest productivity was during his stay in New York from 1880 until he returned to Cuba to die on the battlefield against the Spaniards in 1895.

In New York he was what we would today call a "free-lance" as well as an "in-house" translator. He translated several books for the publishing house of D. Appleton, and did a series of translations for newspapers. As a revolutionary activist in Cuba's long struggle for independence he translated into English a number of articles and pamphlets supporting that movement.

There was clearly a dichotomy in Martí's feeling about the kind of work he was translating. Like many professionals, he undertook for money translation tasks which had little intellectual or emotional appeal for him. De la Cuesta illustrates this nicely with a quotation in which Martí reflects on his translation projects in February 1883, writing to his sister Amelia: "Anoche puse fin a la traducción de un libro de lógica que me ha parecido - a pesar de tener yo por maravillosamente inútiles tantas reglas pueriles - preciosísimo libro, puesto que con el producto de su traducción puedo traer a mi padre a mi lado."

Martí was also a diplomat in his years in exile in New York, acting as consul for several Latin America countries and conducting their business in that city as well as at various conferences in Washington. He wrote for the major newspaper *La Nación* of Buenos Aires, and his candid commentaries for that paper during the 1889-1890 First Inter-American Conference in Washington provide a neat counterbalance to the dry official documentation. Martí obviously had access to behind-the-scenes sources (especially from the Argentine side), and his columns were sprinkled with almost gossipy references to what the various delegations said to (and about) each other in private. His commentary on the strains between the host US delegation and the aggressively independent Argentine delegation are especially illuminating.[84]

Martí was much involved in writing for Spanish-speaking audiences about the assassination attempt and eventual death of President Garfield in 1881. Using several New York newspapers as sources, Martí took the basic accounts and translated them, but also added personal touches which in his view were necessary to convey the appropriate emotional tone to a Latin audience.[85] In so doing he showed his skill as a translator as well as his creative abilities as a journalist and author.

Although Martí never presented a systematic theory of translation nor did he write extensively about his approach to translation, he did jot down occasional thoughts on the subject which are of value: "yo creo que traducir es transpensar ... traducir es pensar en español lo que en su idioma ellos (los autores) pensaron ... traducir es estudiar, analizar, ahondar." His awareness of the translator's dilemma of the faithful versus the beautiful is evidenced in his belief that "la traducción debe ser natural para que parezca como si el libro hubiese sido escrito en la lengua al que lo traduces, que en esto se conocen las buenas traducciones" and "ve pues el cuidado con que hay que traducir, para que la traducción pueda entenderse y resulte elegante - y para que el libro no quede, como tantos libros traducidos, en la misma lengua extraña en que estaba."[86]

B. TRANSLATION TIDBIT.

An American technician working in Russia received the following upsetting telegram regarding his only daughter back home: "Harriet hung for juvenile crimes." It turned out that the telegram had been translated from English into Russian and then back to English. The original text was "Harriet suspended for minor offenses."[87]

C. THEORY OF TRANSLATION.

Language interferences: Anglicisms in Spanish.

Languages affect each other, and languages in direct geographic contact can significantly change each other's lexicon, phonology, syntax and style.[88] There is usually a dominant and a subordinate language, depending on the inherent characteristics of each language and the political and cultural circumstances. For example, the language spoken in the capital of an imperial power will exercise strong influences on those other languages within the sphere of influence of the empire. Border areas are especially prolific areas for language interaction, as are linguistic enclaves within a nation. As noted in the Lesson on comparative aspects of English and Spanish, the two languages have strengths (and weaknesses) in certain features. Thus, Spanish is better suited for emotional expression, such as in poetry and speeches, while English is perhaps more appropriate for science, technology and business. Therefore, one would expect English to penetrate Spanish in matters of science and technology, especially when the pioneering research and development work in a particular field takes place using the English language or in U.S. laboratories or factories.

Languages can also be in contact through mass media. The widespread dissemination of U.S. movies and television programs throughout the Spanish-speaking world has linguistic impact, although this is lessened by the custom of dubbing the dialogue into Spanish. But even with dubbing, the cultural aspects make themselves known, and dubbing frequently carries over into the TL certain features of the SL. This problem has a political impact in

Latin America, where the perceived penetrations by U.S. media are frequently labelled "cultural imperialism."

The translator has a special role and responsibility in this matter of languages in contact. Since the translator is a bilingual and bicultural individual, s/he is frequently a conduit for new influences to cross over from one language to the next. Although all good translators are careful not to allow this to happen to any significant degree, it is all too easy to let certain SL linguistic features enter into the TL through translation, many times with the translator not even being aware of it. This is especially true for the more subtle aspects of language, such as style and tone. New forms of words and grammatical constructions are more obvious, and generally the translator will spot them.

The problem of the translator serving as conduit for language interference is more serious if the translator lacks ability or confidence in the language s/he is translating **into**. This is yet another reason why translators should only go into their mother tongue, and should do all they can to improve their writing ability in their native language. When one translates into one's second tongue, one is never as certain about grammar, style (and even lexicon) as when going into the mother tongue, and this situation then permits a greater degree of language interference.

Anglicisms in the Spanish language have long been a sensitive issue for those who wish to protect their Hispanic heritage.[89] When Spain was the dominant political and cultural power in Europe, this was not perceived to be a problem. But in the past several centuries the Hispanic world has felt unduly influenced by the Anglo-Saxon one, and an annoying and threatening aspect of this influence has been the penetration of the Spanish language by English. Spain's Real Academia de la Lengua has strongly resisted Anglicisms, and will consistently coin and suggest proper Spanish words, usually with a Latin root, to be used in place of the Anglicism. At times this works, but all too often the new Spanish word is used only in restricted academic and intellectual circles, while at the popular level of colloquial talk and mass media the Anglicism dominates.

The difficulties that Spanish has in resisting Anglicisms can be illustrated with the word "feedback." This term originated in the field of audio communications engineering, and was defined as the effect of a small portion of an amplifier's output finding its way back to the input side and thus feeding on itself. The phenomenon is readily observed when a microphone is placed too close to a speaker, and a loud squealing results. By extension, the term now has come to also mean a response or reaction to some action, such as a political speech, a publishing venture or a policy proposal. The Real Academia proposed the Spanish term "retroalimentación," which is awkward and ungainly, as well as suggesting rather bizarre feeding habits. It has gained some acceptance in the technical engineering usage, but not in the broader sense of feedback to a speech or some other form of human expression. In the long run "retroalimentación" is likely to be used less and less and "feedback" will have the field to itself. The same phenomenon is also evident in the computer field, where the English language's capacity to create compound words and string together nouns and adjectives is clearly more efficient and descriptive than Spanish, which has a need to insert prepositions and articles. Consider these terms:
"software" = "programas y sistemas para la computadora"
"data processing" = "procesamiento de datos"
"hardware" = "el equipo y las maquinarias de las computadoras."

The problem of coining technical and scientific words in Spanish is not as severe if the English relies on words with Latin or Greek roots, since then the Spanish can legitimately coin a similar word from the same Latin or Greek root and avoid the direct acceptance of an Anglicism. Such is the case with words like "televisión," "micrófono," and "transistor." Many medical and scientific terms follow systematic naming procedures which respect these Greek and Latin roots, and are therefore not offensive.

The phenomenon of Anglicisms penetrating Spanish is more obvious in the spoken than the written Spanish, and more at the casual or slang level of speech than at the more formal and academic. Thus, the most blatant examples of Anglicisms in Spanish are observed in street slang along the cities of the US-Mexican border, in the region around Miami, in Puerto Rico, and in the Hispanic barrios of many large cities of the U.S. The easy penetration of English into Spanish is facilitated by the fact that many of the Hispanics accepting the Anglicisms have an inadequate academic foundation in their own Spanish mother tongue, especially in its written form, and thus find it difficult to resist the power of the Anglicism. It is common to hear words like "troca," "parquear," "yonque," "nursa," "typear." These tend to alarm the purists of the Spanish language, but their movement from spoken street slang to formal written Spanish is a long and slow one, and many of them will never make it. Dictionaries, and especially the formidable *Diccionario de la Real Academia Española*, tend to run several years behind the general acceptance of a word in written Spanish, and a word's inclusion requires careful scrutiny to see if any acceptable Spanish coinage has a chance of resisting the Anglicism.

There are many different categories of Anglicisms in the lexical, grammatical and stylistic areas of linguistics. García Yebra lists these as being among the more significant:
- Misuse of prepositions
- Improper word order
- English words or variants accepted too readily into Spanish
- Incorrect use of Spanish "que" under the influence of "that"
- Excessive use of the passive voice in Spanish
- Unnatural conciseness
- Redundancy (not as common as conciseness)
- Wrong verb forms, or their improper use.

Application: The translator must be aware that Anglicisms exist, since s/he may encounter them in the Spanish, but must resist being a conduit for their entry into written Spanish.

D. TRANSLATION PROBLEMS AND TECHNIQUES.

Anglicisms in Spanish.

As suggested in the Theory section above, the translator must be on guard against carrying over English words, grammar, and other language features into Spanish when translating. Some examples of the most common kinds of Anglicisms in Spanish are given below.

Lexical. These are fairly obvious to the native speaker of Spanish, since s/he is generally aware that the word in question sounds "foreign," and that there is a more correct and acceptable Spanish word available. The translator frequently introduces this type of Anglicism into Spanish because the word has a similar word in English; this is the old problem of false or partially false cognates. Some examples:

"he went to the funeral service"
    Anglicism: "asistió al servicio funeral"
    Better: "asistió al servicio fúnebre"
"there is much atmospheric pollution"
    Anglicism: "hay mucha polución atmosférica"
    Better: "hay mucha contaminación ambiental"
"he said hello to María"
    Anglicism: "le dijo hola a María"
    Better: "le saludó a María"
"the house is located on the corner"
    Anglicism: "la casa está localizada en la esquina"
    Better: "la casa está ubicada en la esquina"
"it is an industry standard"
    Anglicism: "es un estándar de la industria"
    Better: "es una norma de la industria"
"his film is just out"
    Anglicism: "su film acaba de salir"
    Better: "su película acaba de estrenar"
"the president was inaugurated yesterday"
    Anglicism: "el Presidente se inauguró ayer"
    Better: "el Presidente tomó posesión ayer"
"he played a key role"
    Anglicism: "jugó un rol llave"
    Better: "desempeñó un papel fundamental"
"he forgot the topic of the lecture"
    Anglicism: "olvidó el tópico de la lectura"
    Better: "olvidó el tema de la conferencia."

Syntactical. These Anglicisms result from carrying English grammatical structures over into Spanish. They are more subtle and difficult to spot than the lexical ones because the prime reader may be vaguely aware that the translated text seems odd or foreign, but not know why unless a detailed grammatical analysis is made. Many of these are listed as "pitfalls" in Holt's text *1001 Pitfalls in Spanish*. Some of the more common ones include:

- Making proper names plural:
"The Johnsons live here"
    Anglicism: "Los Johnsones viven aquí"
    Better: "Los Johnson viven aquí"

- Overuse of possessive pronouns with parts of the body:
"Please fasten your seat belts"
    Anglicism: "Favor de abrocharse sus cinturones de seguridad"
    Better: "Favor de abrocharse los cinturones de seguridad"
"My arm hurts"
    Anglicism: "me duele mi brazo"
    Better: "me duele el brazo"

- Making decades plural:
"The sixties were the period of Camelot"
    Anglicism: "los sesentas eran la época de Camelot"
    Better: "los sesenta eran la época de Camelot"

- Incorrect use of adverbs: "He organized it rapidly and efficiently"
    Anglicism: "lo organizó rápidamente y eficazmente"
    Better: "lo organizó rápida y eficazmente."

Interference by frequency of Anglicisms. Another form of English penetration into Spanish is by overuse of words and constructions which are acceptable in Spanish, but to a degree that is not normal and begins to sound "foreign" to the native-speaking prime reader. Each sentence taken by itself is correct, but put together into paragraphs and pages the end result seems odd. Excessive use of the passive construction in Spanish is one obvious example. Another would be the excessive use of personal pronouns

which are not needed much in Spanish because the verb form indicates the person:
"Yo quiero comer"; better: "quiero comer."

Conceptual Anglicisms. Finally, ideas or concepts which are imbedded in Anglo-Saxon culture may have perfectly acceptable translations into Spanish which are grammatically and lexically correct, but which are Anglicisms because they undergo a change in meaning when inserted into the TL culture. For example, an historical reference to the "Paris Peace Treaty" would mean to most U.S. citizens the 1783 Treaty which ended the U.S. Revolutionary War. But to a Spaniard or Cuban it would most probably seem like a reference to the treaty which ended the Spanish-American War of 1898.

E. COGNATES.

fc = false cognate   pc = partial cognate (be careful)
pfc = partial false cognate (be very careful)

LUJURIA (fc) ≠ luxury; instead use "lujo."
        = lust, lewdness, physical excess, voluptuousness.
MANDATARIO (fc) ≠ manadatory; instead use "obligatorio."
        = governor or political head:
"el primer mandatario George Bush."
MANERAS (pfc) = way of doing something.
        ≠ good habits or manners; instead use "modales."
MANIFESTACION (fc) ≠ manifestation; instead use "expresión."
        = demonstration, especially political:
"organizaron la manifestación en frente de la OEA."
MATRIMONIO (pfc) ≠ matrimony as a legal state.
        = married couple: "el matrimonio Pérez vive aquí."
MEDITERRANEO (pfc) = the Mediterranean Sea.
        Also = landlocked: "Paraguay es país mediterráneo."
MISERIA (pfc) = poverty: "vive en la miseria - no tiene nada."
        ≠ suffering; instead use "dolor" or "sufrimiento."
MODALIDAD (pfc) = modality in a diplomatic sense.
        For other meanings use: method, way, means, approach.

F. PROVERBS AND IDIOMS.

Hacer puente   A three day weekend. To take the intervening
     workday off (Friday or Monday) to make a four day weekend.
Hacerse ilusiones   To dream; build castles in Spain.
Hay moros en la costa   The coast is not clear;
     there is something going on; be careful.
Hecho a medida   Made to order.
Incorporarse a   To join (a group).
Ir a medias   To split; go fifty-fifty.
Ir al grano   To get to the point.
La esperanza es lo último que se pierde.   Hope springs eternal.
La experiencia es madre de la ciencia.
     Experience is the best teacher.
La mujer y el vidrio siempre están en peligro.
     Glasses and lasses are brittle ware.

Figure 15-1. José Martí.

LESSON 16

A. HISTORY OF TRANSLATION.

Translation at the turn of the Century.

The Victorian translators at the turn of the century in England developed a peculiar tendency to archaize, which is to render the foreign text into English in such a way as to try and convey a sense of distant time and place. The technique was to use a mock antique language, which sounded very unusual in English, in order to try to carry the reader back to the original setting of the text in the source language. The end result was artificial and even pedantic, and tended to restrict the products of translation to a relatively small intellectual elite. From a theoretical perspective it was the exact opposite of the frequently stated principle that a translation ought to sound natural in the target language, so that it should not read like a translation. The Victorian translators' justification for this procedure was to convey a sense of the original, as awkward as this might be in contemporary English.[90]

Diplomatic translation received more attention in the late 19th Century. Secretary Hamilton Fish had reorganized the U.S. State Department in 1870, setting up a Translating Department, although it was staffed with only one permanent translator. By 1910 the Department grew as communications were received in as many as 13 languages. Most of this material consisted of messages from foreign governments, treaties, and the proceedings of international conferences. Interpreting was not given much priority, since it was assumed that any serious diplomat would be able to conduct his business in French.

The need for translators in the U.S. State Department was heightened by the fact that very few of our diplomats spoke any foreign languages except for French, which was still the standard language of diplomacy up to the First World War. U.S. diplomats assigned to Spain or Latin America were generally deficient in their language skills. Roland[91] tells several anecdotes concerning Ambassador Henry Lane Wilson and how he fared in his Latin American assignments with his limited Spanish. Shortly after the War of the Pacific between Peru and Chile (1879-1883) Wilson was on board a ship to Santiago, Chile where he was to be the new ambassador. His ship made a stop at Callao, Peru, and the Peruvian government, assuming Wilson was the US ambassador to Peru, gave him an elaborate welcoming ceremony. Wilson's Spanish was inadequate to tell them of their mistake, and when the Peruvian authorities finally learned that they had been honoring the US Ambassador to Chile there was "a considerable cooling of their courtesy." Wilson later illustrated the value of the rule that a little linguistic knowledge is a dangerous thing when he said, at a diplomatic reception, that his wife could speak "español mejor si no tuviera medias." He meant to say she could speak "español mejor si no tuviera miedo."

B. TRANSLATION TIDBIT.
Two translated advertisements:[92]
"Take one of our horse-drive city tours. We guarantee no miscarriages."
"The comfort of the ride based on the suspension, plus the front-wheel traction amazes virgin passengers."

C. THEORY OF TRANSLATION.

Language interferences: hispanicisms in English.

For a number of historical, political and cultural reasons the problem of Spanish interference into English (hispanicisms) is much less severe than that of anglicisms into Spanish. Nevertheless, hispanicisms in English are very notable in certain areas of the United States, such as the U.S.-Mexican border, Southern Florida, and certain neighborhoods of large cities in the Northeast. It also poses a problem for the person whose first language is Spanish and who lives or works in an environment where English is the dominant language. An excessive use of hispanicisms by such a person tends to make him or her seem foreign and may have unfortunate side effects such as discrimination or limitations in job or social possibilities. As Carney has noted, the speaking of "Spanglish" is not viewed kindly by academics, supervisors and language purists in either English or Spanish.[93]

    This is not to imply that hispanicisms (or anglicisms) should be seen as negative. They can enrich a target culture by means of linguistic resources imported from a source culture. This aspect is especially valuable and justified when the transfer is at the lexical level and is tied to an object or category which does not exist in the target culture. Over the centuries Spanish has made many lexical contributions to English, and continues to do so. Some of these contributions have been directly from Spanish words, and in other cases Spanish has served as the conduit for words which originated in other languages with a special relationship to Spanish, such as Arabic and the Indian languages of the New World. Things and customs which originated in the Spanish-speaking world, (such as bullfighting, typical dances, special foods) are also obvious generators of hispanicisms in English. Some words have special historical significance, such as "guerrilla" (the word used by Napoleon's forces to describe the way the Spanish fought in the Peninsular War), or the term "fifth column" which as "quinta columna" was used by a Spanish Civil War general to label his covert supporters in Madrid as he laid seige to it. Many geographic place names in the United States have Spanish origins as a legacy of the time when these regions were under Spanish or Mexican control, or as indicators that Hispanic explorers passed that way. Pei notes, for example that three dangerous rocks on the Alaskan coast bear the names Abreojo, Alárgate, and Quita Sueño.[94]

    Hispanicisms are also very evident in the language of expatriate English-speaking persons living in a Spanish-speaking nation. A prime example is the Anglo community residing in several South American nations, most notably Argentina, Uruguay and Chile. These individuals are now up to fourth and fifth generation citizens of their country of residence, but maintain British customs and speak an English that has become hispanicized to some degree at both the lexical and syntactic level. There is also a sub-language (frequently used for humorous effect) which deliberately exaggerates the hispanicisms to the point where the English is difficult for an outsider to understand. For many years the **Buenos Aires Herald** ran a regular column in which a ficticious character "Ramón" wrote a series of letters in this style. Here is an excerpt from the collection of columns, which were published as a book in 1979 (note from the fourth paragraph that "Ramón" studied to be a translator):[95]

I supplicate you that you pass of high so much discourtesy of my part for not writing these past four months.

What passed was that I had planned to go to that one in person and because of that I desisted. It had the object my visit to see if I could acomodate myself in some ministry or gobernation after they happened the events that are of public domination.

But in vespers of absenting myself there writes me a friend of the faculty to tell me that my voyage would be to the divine button because the things have not changed themselves nothing: the milics have copated themselves everything.

As you can wait, I felt myself disillusioned, because I give myself count that this life of camp doesn't fall me well, and of commerce I do not want to occupy myself. For me, who coursed three years of studies of public traducer there should exist entry into the official life. With the patience of always, I will wait.

By disgrace I have had to occupy myself more to depth with the matters of the cows. Disgracefully the past week, he died himself the capataz. He had 78 and was born, created himself and worked here all one life. They received sepulture his rests here on the proper estancia.

...

...

For the rest, the things go as always. The old one has reposed himself of the broken leg and is occupying himself newly of the things. But he and Ramoncito don't see each other well. The old one doesn't tolerate the discs of the Beatles and the long hair of Ramoncito, and when he is not feeling too good he arms the great one. Esther dedicates herself to assure the tranquility of the house. Of passing, she asks that I send you her salutes to the which I aggregate a great embrace from your friend.

RAMON.

D. TRANSLATION PROBLEMS AND TECHNIQUES.

Hispanicisms in English.

To illustrate the significance of hispanicisms in English, we will "back-translate" Ramon's letter into the Spanish in which he conceived the letter. Notice how the "English" really is almost a word-for-word transliteration from Spanish, complete with lexical and syntactical hispanicisms. Some of Ramon's writing also includes Argentine slang expressions or words, which are listed here to avoid confusion:

al divino botón = useless
los milicos = the military
se han copado= have grabbed
los asuntos de las vacas = the matters dealing with cattle
el viejo = the father
no se ven bien = don't see eye to eye
se arma la grande = there is a big fuss

Le suplico que pases por alto la gran descortesía por mi parte al no escribir estos últimos cuatro meses.

Lo que pasó es que había planeado ir en persona y por eso desistí. Tenía el objeto mi visita de ver si me podía acomodar en algún ministerio o gobernación después de que ocurrieron los eventos que son de dominio público.

Pero en vísperas de ausentarme me escribe un amigo de la facultad para decirme que mi viaje sería al divino botón porque las cosas no se han cambiado en nada: los milicos se han copado todo para ellos mismos.

Como puedes esperar, me sentí desilusionado, porque me di cuenta que esta vida de campo no me cae bien, y de comercio no me quiero ocupar. Para mí, que cursé tres años de estudios de traductor público, debería existir entrada en la vida oficial. Con la paciencia de siempre, esperaré.

Por desgracia he tenido que ocuparme más a fondo con los asuntos de las vacas. Desgraciadamente la semana pasada, se murió el capataz. Tenía 78 y nació, se crió y trabajó aquí toda una vida. Sus restos recibieron sepultura aquí en la propia estancia.
...

...

Por lo demás, todo va como siempre. El viejo se ha repuesto de la pierna rota y se está ocupando nuevamente de las cosas. Pero él y Ramoncito no se ven bien. El viejo no aguanta los discos de los Beatles y el pelo largo de Ramoncito, y cuando no se siente muy bien se arma la grande. Esther se dedica a asegurar la tranquilidad de la casa. De paso, me pide que te mande su saludo, a lo cual le agrego un gran abrazo de tu amigo.

RAMON.

E. COGNATES.

fc = false cognate   pc = partial cognate (be careful)
pfc = partial false cognate (be very careful)

MOLESTAR (pfc) = to bother: "Pedro está molestando al gato."
    ≠ sexually abuse;
    instead use: "abusar sexualmente" or "violar" (rape).
MOROSO (fc) = default, as on a loan.
    ≠ in bad humor; instead use "malhumorado," "hosco."
MOTIVO (pfc) = motive as in ground or cause for something:
    "motivo de divorcio."
    ≠ motive as in reason for a crime; instead use "móvil."
NATIVO (pfc) = adjective as in "native language."
    ≠ noun "native" as in "a native of Mexico";
    instead use "natural": "es natural de Mexico."
NEGOCIAR (pfc) = negotiate in a diplomatic sense, but in general
    usage means to discuss or talk over, without necessarily
    having a legal commitment.
NOMBRAMIENTO (pfc) = naming a person to fill an appointment.
    But for nominating someone use "proponer como candidato."
NOTICIA (fc) ≠ notice; instead use "aviso."
    = news. In singular means "a piece of news":
    "una noticia interesante."
    In plural means "the news": "escuchó las noticias."
NOTORIO (pfc) = well-known, famous in a neutral or positive way.
    ≠ well-known for negative reasons;
    instead use "de mala fama."

OCASION (pfc) = occasion in the sense of "opportunity,"
not in the sense of "event."
For "event," instead use "suceso," or "acontecimiento."
Also = sale or bargain: "gran ocasión - venta a medio precio."

F. PROVERBS AND IDIOMS.

La necesidad hace maestro.   Necessity is the mother of invention.
Levantar la mesa   To clear the table.
Llevar a cabo   To carry out.
Llevarse bien con   To get along well with.
Lo de menos   That's the least of it.
Los niños y los borrachos siempre dicen la verdad.
     Out of the mouths of babes and sucklings. In vino veritas.
Manos a la obra   Let's get to work.
Matar dos pájaros de un tiro   Kill two birds with one stone.

Figure 16-1. Deep meaning.

LESSON 17

A. HISTORY OF TRANSLATION.

Walter Owen: Translator of South American Epics.

This Scot transplanted to the Argentine Pampas stands as a fitting symbol of how the translator can open up a key aspect of a culture to readers in another language. Born in Glasgow, he spent much of his boyhood in Montevideo and as an adult returned to the River Plate area to work as a stockbroker. He thus had the opportunity to become bicultural as well as bilingual, and applied his skill to the translation into English of the major epic poems of the Southern part of South America. In so doing his objective was not simply esthetic, but cultural and even political in terms of bringing closer together the English-speaking peoples and those of Latin America. As he put it, he hoped that his work "in its modest way may advance between peoples of different speech, the friendly interchange of thought and feeling which is the foundation of mutual esteem and the surest establishment for good fellowship. To have done so is the best reward of the translator."[96] In his preface to *Martín Fierro* he expressed the same idea in verse:

> pa que el gaucho inglés sepa lo que el
> gaucho argentino era;
> y el argentino que el inglés
> también es gaucho a su manera.

What Owen did was to "English" (his verb for translate) the principal epics of the part of Latin America he knew best: José Hernández' *Martín Fierro*, Alonso de Ercilla y Zúñiga's *La Araucana*, and Zorrilla de San Martín's *Tabaré*, among others. In so doing he made available to the English-speaking world these neglected masterpieces of the Southern Cone. But as a translator he felt obliged to tell his readers (in extensive introductions or prefaces) how he crafted his works of translation. Thus, his legacy is a double one, of considerable value to both the reader of epic Latin American poetry as well as to the student of translation.

Owen avoided excessively literal translations, realizing that they would be of little interest to the reader trying to understand the gaucho or araucanian culture. He was willing to sacrifice what he called "verbal accuracy" (i.e., word for word rendition) in order to achieve clarity and ease of style. His ultimate goal was what we would call "equivalent impact": "it must produce upon the consciousness of the reader an equivalent total impression to that produced by the original work upon readers in whose vernacular it was written."[97] He reiterates this philosophy in his preface to the translation of La Araucana: "Translations of poems which adhere faithfully to the original text yield small pleasure to the reader, and what value they have is for the student of philology or semantics.... I consider the translation of poetry into poetry a liberal art and not an exact science .... To coin a portmanteau-term for this sort of translation, it might be called a psychological transvernacularisation."[98]

Here is his "transvernacularisation" of the opening stanza:

Aquí me pongo a cantar	I sit me here to sing my song
Al compás de la vigüela	To the beat of my old guitar;
Que el hombre lo desvela	To the man whose life is a bitter cup,
Una pena estrordinaria	With a song may yet his heart lift up,
Como la ave solitaria	As the lonely bird on a leafless tree,
Con el cantar se consuela	That sings 'neath the gloaming star.

In the preface to the translation of **La Araucana**, Owen invites the reader to share with him the intimate details of the process by which he takes the original poem of the Chilean conquest, makes a first rough semi-literal translation, and then plays with each line, word, and syllable to achieve the translation which most closely conveys the spirit, meaning and rhythm of the 16th Century Spanish original. This preface stands as one of the most complete explanations which a poet-translator has ever given of the intricacies of his work. He modestly says: "It will not be foreign to the purpose of these introductory remarks and will perhaps be of some entertainment to my readers if I illustrate the working of the system I have outlined, as applied to the opening stanza of Ercilla's epic. I will first give the original Spanish text of the stanza, then my first roughly literal translation, followed by a running commentary showing the development of the finished English version."[99]

The Spanish original by Alonso de Ercilla, 1569:
No las damas, amor, no gentilezas,
De caballeros canto enamorados,
Ni las muestras, regalos y ternezas
De amorosos afectos y cuidados;
Mas el valor, los hechos, las proezas
De aquellos españoles esforzados,
Que a la cerviz de Arauco no domada
Pusieron duro yugo por la espada.

Owen's first "approximately literal translation" (early 1900's):
Not ladies, love, nor courtesies
Of amorous knights I sing,
Nor tokens, sweets, and favours
Of love's delights and cares;
But the valour, deeds, and exploits
Of those stalwart Spaniards,
That on Arauco's untamed neck
Placed by a sword a rigorous yoke.

Owen notes that this first cut carries the sense of the original, but that the "rhythm and ring and martial tramp of Ercilla are absent. The epic note is wanting; the bird of poetry has escaped our net of English words. No patching or mending of the new form will recapture the spirit of the original. What the translator has to do is to mentally digest this raw material, and once it is well assimilated, imagine himself Ercilla, seated quill in hand in old Madrid about the third quarter of the sixteenth century, with a clean sheet before him and his portfolio of manuscript notes at hand, ruminating the opening lines of his epic of the Araucan wars."[100]

Owen proceeds to do just that for six pages of his preface, showing the reader in great detail how he arrives at his final version:
Sing, Muse: but not of Venus and her chuck,
And amorous jousts in dainty lists of love,
Favours and forfeits won in Beauty's siege

By soft assaults of chamber gallantry;
But of the valiant deeds and worthy fame
Of those who far on surge-ensundered shores,
Bent the proud neck of Araucania's race
To Spain's stern yoke, by war's arbitrament.

B. TRANSLATION TIDBIT.
Two observations by the Bible translator Eugene Nida:[101]
    At least some portion of the Bible has been translated into 1,457 languages, with 253 languages having the entire Bible, and 330 more having the entire New Testament. These languages are understood by 98% of the world's population. The remaining 2% speak an additional 1,000 languages (estimated).
    In the Bolivian Quechua language a very good term for Lord, "Apu," is not employed in Bible translation because in the grammatical object form it must be used with the suffix "-ta." The resulting word, "Aputa" has an unfortunate resemblance to a vulgar Spanish word.

C. THEORY OF TRANSLATION.

The Untranslatables: Idioms, Metaphors, Folklore.

    There is a category of language forms which are so culture-bound and culture-specific as to defy translation by routine methods. These are the idiomatic expressions, metaphors (and their variants) and that collection of proverbs, word plays and sayings which could be catalogued as linguistic "folklore." The problem with these forms is that they are so deeply rooted in their original culture that their deep meaning has little if any relation to their surface structures, and may in fact be unique to the culture that produced them. There is also the case of common words which have apparently valid cognates in other languages, but which turn out on closer examination to have been changed by each culture in such ways that to use them as valid cognates is a mistake. The case of the word "democracy" is a good example; it is fair to say that each nation's political culture defines the concept of "democracy" in its own way, and members of that nation tend to apply their concept to the "democracy" in other nations. The German Democratic Republic, the U.S. Democratic National Committee, the National Endowment for Democracy (U.S.) and the Christian Democratic Party of El Salvador all use the word in their institutional title, but clearly the meaning changes if we try to isolate the concept or remove it from the milieu of its particular political culture.

The problem of these untranslatables has given rise to the theoretical notion of "equivalence," which argues that, with few exceptions, it ought to be possible to find equivalent structures for these untranslatables in SL and TL. Since these linguistic forms are "semantic novelties,"[102] we must be willing to sacrifice stylistic or formal equivalencies in favor of the dynamic or functional equivalencies. Pragmatism, in other words, should be the governing factor; whatever produces the closest effect in the TL is the form that should be used regardless of wide differences in the lexicon or syntax.

Idiomatic expressions are the most common form of these "untranslatables." An idiom is a figure of speech involving at least two words which cannot be understood literally, and whose meaning is carried by the words as a unit, not individually. The error in attempting a literal translation should be obvious. The deep meaning can only be given by the actual usage in the culture involved. Some examples in English and Spanish: a laughing matter; according to Hoyle; birds of a feather; Dutch treat; a grandes rasgos; a la Americana; carne de gallina; dar una mano; el árbol de la ciencia.

Metaphors and similes are both figurative comparisons of one thing to another. In a metaphor we speak of one thing as if it were another and characterize it indirectly in the process: John is a rock in this time of trouble; the problem is a bear; the troops were swaying fields of wheat; he bought the farm in Vietnam. In a simile the comparison is done more directly using the word "like" or "as": as cool as a cucumber; like an anchor in a storm; he swam like a fish. The structure of metaphors and similes consists of a topic and then a comment about the topic. The topic itself poses no special translation problems, but the comment on the topic usually grows in different ways in different cultures, making an exact translation difficult. In fact, the comparison may involve things or concepts that do not exist in the target language culture or its language. For example, when translating the simile "as pure as snow" into Indian languages of the Amazon Basin there is frequently no word for snow available because it is outside of the tribe's experience. But the topic or notion of whiteness is known, and the best solution then is to find something which that particular culture uses as the comparison in an equivalent simile. In the case of several Amazon tribes that equivalent simile was found to be clouds or the feathers of a bird.

Other problems are caused by the comparison having a different value in different cultures. For example, the English metaphor "he is an ox" connotes strength and massive size. But in the culture of an Argentine gaucho it connotes an emasculated, passive and not very smart animal -- hardly a compliment. A useful technique when dealing with metaphors is to reduce them to similes, which are generally clearer in structure. Once this is done, then the translator searches his own memory bank for a dynamically equivalent simile in the target language (if none is found the translator can consult with colleagues or native speakers). In the case of the metaphor "he is an ox" we could proceed to convert it into a simile ("he is strong like an ox") and see what simile in Argentine gaucho Spanish carries the same dynamic equivalent of strength; the answer would be something like "tan fuerte como un caballo." If none is found, it might be necessary to abandon the simile and metaphor, and simply state the quality without any comparison: "era muy fuerte." The meaning has been conveyed, although with a significant loss in the color and elegance of the expression.

The category of proverb and popular saying is usually even more deeply rooted in the culture, although here too it is frequently possible to find formal equivalencies, and if not, then to find dynamic equivalencies which convey the same impression or impact. Expletives, oaths and swear words are a special category which must be approached carefully to avoid sounding ludicrous or excessively offensive. The principle of pragmatic dynamic equivalence should reign supreme here, and if there is any doubt a native speaker should be consulted to accurately measure the impact.

D. TRANSLATION PROBLEMS AND TECHNIQUES.

<u>Metaphors, Idioms and Proverbs.</u>

These "untranslatables" are deeply rooted in individual cultures, and require that the translator totally abandon any attempt to translate literally word-for-word. Instead, s/he should adhere completely to the concept of dynamic equivalence, seeking the TL expression which has the same impact on the prime reader as the SL original would have on a native speaker of the SL.

Metaphors. Larson[103] has several useful techniques for dealing with metaphors. The first is a three-step process by which metaphor is changed to simile using the words "as" or "like". Following this the comparison is made explicit so as to avoid any possible misunderstanding. To use the ox metaphor as an example:
English metaphor: John is an ox. Simile: John is like an ox. Explicit simile: John is as strong as an ox. The explicit equivalent simile: John es tan fuerte como un caballo. (Note that the ox, at least in Argentine gaucho Spanish, has an image of being emasculated, slow and dumb; this is not the appropriate image, so "horse" is chosen instead as being the dynamic equivalent). Spanish simile: John es como un caballo. Spanish metaphor: John es un caballo.
A second Larson approach is a five-step hierarchy:
1. Keep the metaphor if the TL permits it (i.e., if the equivalent metaphor has the same dynamic effect).
2. If not, change it to a simile and translate.
3. As an alternate, a different metaphor in the TL may be selected if it has the same dynamic impact.
4. Or, the metaphor may be kept and the meaning explained.
5. Finally, the meaning of the metaphor may be translated without keeping the image of a metaphor or simile.
Using our ox metaphor as an example:
1. Juan es un buey (this is not good because of the different image attached to "buey").
2. Juan es tan fuerte como un buey (better but still not good because although we have made explicit the strength of the "buey," there are other less desirable features of the "buey" in Spanish).
3. Juan es un caballo (good solution using a different metaphor).

4. Juan es un buey porque el buey es un animal muy fuerte (possible but awkward and we still have the problems of the "buey's" other characteristics).

5. Juan es fuerte (we have kept the meaning but lost the imagery).

One final piece of advice for the translator dealing with a metaphor is to see if the solution "works" (i.e., does it really achieve the same dynamic equivalent effect). If it does not, then s/he should proceed down Larson's scale of choices until a solution is found that does indeed "work." The higher up the scale the solution stays, the more elegant and effective the translation will be. But the ultimate criteria remains: if it doesn't "work," don't use it.

Idiomatic expressions have special meanings derived from the cultures they come from. When translated word-for-word they can be either meaningless, seem foreign, or create other problems. For example, the English idiomatic expression "give me a light" for a cigarette cannot be translated word for word as "déme luz" because there is a very close idiomatic expression, "dar a luz," which means to give birth. The more appropriate expression is "déme fuego." English tends to use a lot of compound words, which are a form of idiom; Spanish resists this trend and instead requires prepositions to tie various noun strings together, or else coins a new word. Idiomatic expressions are hard to deal with because they must be memorized or looked up as idioms (and not separate words) in special dictionaries.[104]

Proverbs. Examples of these are given in Section F of each Lesson of this text. Proverbs tend to be strongly linked to folk-culture, especially rural. It is common to find rough dynamic equivalent proverbs across cultures when describing common features of the human experience (birth, love, marriage, occupation, personality features, physical characteristics, good and bad luck, etc). Duff, in his *Third Language* book,[105] makes the interesting point that the euphony (the sound and rhythm of a proverb) gives it much of its "punch," and that this is what is lost when making a literal translation. He notes for example the difference between a proverb, such as "an apple a day keeps the doctor away," and a re-written version in prose which is bland and uninspiring: "if you eat an apple every day you will be healthy and will not need a doctor so often." This version would be an example of his "third language," which may contain the meaning, but is not an effective translation.

E. COGNATES.

fc = false cognate   pc = partial cognate (be careful)
pfc = partial false cognate (be very careful)

OCURRENCIA (fc) ≠ event; use "suceso" or "acontecimiento."
    = witticism or clever saying.
OFICIAL (pfc) = adjective "official": "una carta oficial."
    As noun = military officer.
    As noun ≠ official; instead use "funcionario."
OFICIO (fc) ≠ office; instead use "oficina."
    = occupation or job, usually manual: "el oficio de carpintero."
OFICIOSO (fc) ≠ officious; instead use "entremetido."
    = diligent, responsible.
ORDINARIO (pfc) = everyday, common.
    Also = vulgar.
ORGANICO (pfc) = organic in the chemical sense.
    Also frequently "ley orgánica" = Constitution of a country.
PAPEL (fc) = writing paper, stationery.
    ≠ a report or research paper; use "trabajo escrito," "ponencia."
PARALIZAR (pfc) = paralyze. Can also mean "freeze" or "suspend":
    "El presidente paralizó las conversaciones con la oposición."

F. PROVERBS AND IDIOMS.
Más bien   Rather.
Más vale pájaro en mano que cien volando.
    A bird in the hand is worth two in the bush.
Más vale prevenir que lamentar.
    An ounce of prevention is worth a pound of cure.
Más vale tarde que nunca.   Better late than never.
Media naranja   Better half; spouse.
Mojado hasta los huesos.   Drenched to the skin, to the bone.
Mucho ojo   Watch out.
Negarse a   To refuse to.

Figure 17-1. Argentine gaucho.

LESSON 18

A. HISTORY OF TRANSLATION.

<u>20th Century Bible Translation.</u>

Translation of the Bible has been the largest single translation project ever undertaken, and for some the project will not be finished until the Bible (or at least the New Testament) is available to every person on earth in his/her own vernacular language. This attitude has linked Christian missionary zeal with the science of linguistics and the practice of translation in ways that have had special significance in Latin America. One example comes from Mexico. The leaders of the Mexican Revolution of 1910 believed that if the Revolution was to survive it had to make a strong effort to bring literacy to the masses of Mexican peasants, many of whom spoke their own Indian languages in preference to the official Spanish language of the country. But most of these Indian languages had no written form, no established rules of grammar, and no literature beyond the oral traditions. The Mexican government's solution was to link forces with Protestant Bible missionary-linguists in a joint endeavor to bring literacy to these Indians.

The key to this process was an American translator-missionary by the name of William Cameron Townsend, who had been working with the Cakchiquel Indians of Mexico since 1917. Although he started as a missionary, he also became a linguist in order to study the Indian languages and translate the Bible into the various languages he came in contact with. To do this he first would study the language, devise an alphabet, analyze the grammar (syntax) and verb structure, then prepare a reading primer in both Spanish and the Indian language. Eventually, using Indian assistants, he would prepare a translation of the Bible in the Indian language, and then move on to the next group of Indians with a different tongue. In the early 1930's, with Mexican government support, he explored the possibility of doing this on a larger scale among the Indians of the Mexican states of Yucatan and Chiapas. Townsend soon realized that his effort would be far more effective if he could train a larger group of linguist-missionaries. This in turn led to the establishment of the Summer Institute of Linguistics at Camp Wycliffe, Arkansas, and the Wycliffe Bible Society.[106]

The name of Wycliffe was selected to honor the English religious reformer John Wycliffe (c. 1330-1384) who had fought against the abuses of the Pope in Rome and argued that Christianity required that every person have direct access to the Bible. Thus, the Bible had to be translated into each vernacular tongue. Wycliffe was an important precursor of the Reformation, and had considerable influence on the ideas of Martin Luther. The Wycliffe Bible (1380-1384) was the first complete translation of the Bible into English, and was an important step in both Bible translation and the Protestant Reformation.

At the Summer Institute of Linguistics Townsend taught his method to an increasingly effective group of American and Latin American linguist-missionaries, who extended their sphere of activity from Mexico to the United States and various other countries of Latin America. From its beginnings in 1935 the Summer Institute of Linguistics has trained linguists and missionaries who have studied over 200 languages, translated the Bible into many of these in 13 different countries, and produced important theoretical and practical linguistic publications in many languages, with significant influence on religion and literacy in these countries. Some of their efforts led to controversy. The established Catholic Church in Latin America has not been pleased at the prospect of Protestant missionaries going into remote areas to study languages, teach literacy, and proselytize by means of Bible translation. Furthermore, since most of the linguist-missionaries are Americans, there is some suspicion, especially strong among the Left in Latin America, that these people are also covert agents of "U.S. imperialism." The Wycliffe Bible Society has attempted to maintain a separate identity from the Summer Institute of Linguistics, but there is a close link between the two institutions, and most of the linguists are also Protestant missionaries. A number of Latin American nations (Brazil, Panama, Mexico and Ecuador among them) have cancelled contracts with the Institute in the past decade for political or religious reasons. In Colombia an Institute member was captured and killed in 1981 by leftist guerrillas, who claimed he was a CIA agent intent on penetrating remote areas of Colombia under the cover of his missionary and translation activity.[107]

B. TRANSLATION TIDBIT.
    One of the most dramatic moments in the history of the United Nations was when Nikita Krushchev of the Soviet Union interrupted a speech by British Prime Minister Harold Macmillan by taking off his shoe and banging it on the table. The unflappable Macmillan responded to Krushchev's crude interruption by remarking: "I'd like that interpreted, if I may."[108]

C. THEORY OF TRANSLATION.

Register, Style, and Tone.

    Within a given language, and even for a single individual, there are different forms of language to be used at different socio-economic levels and situations. Clearly the style, the tone, and the "feel" of the language will be different if the individuals speaking (or writing) are engineers, bus drivers, doctors, students, street people, politicians, spouses, etc. Any one individual in a society speaks with a different style when communicating with one's boss, peers, family, lover, children, cat or dog. The style and tone are also conditioned by the specific circumstances of the communication occasion.

    Linguists refer to these different levels of language as the "register" of the language, and this is important to the translator because s/he must attempt to transfer the same register from SL to TL lest some meaning be lost. According to theorists of language,[109] the principal social factors which determine the register include: age, sex, class, occupation, caste, religion, country of origin, region, schooling, and degree of bilingualism. We can also classify the registers as ranging from the excessively formal (pedantic, jargon), through formal, neutral, casual and vulgar. The range of this register can be illustrated by examples:

Pedantic:	expired	visage	inebriated
Formal:	passed away	countenance	intoxicated
Neutral:	died	face	drunk
Casual:	kicked the bucket	mug	plastered
Vulgar:	croaked	kisser	hammered

In the Lesson on comparative linguistics we observed that English has a tendency to be very concise and even dense because of its ability to string together adjectives and nouns, while Spanish must use a series of prepositional phrases. American English, especially at the upper levels of register (pedantic, jargon and formal) does this to excess, a characteristic which causes some difficulties when translating into Spanish. Thus, a bridge becomes a "load bearing facility," students become "the student body," a book becomes "reading material." The higher registers of Spanish use their own idiosyncratic devices consisting mainly of circumlocution, imagery, and elaborate phraseology which, when translated into English, tend to sound bombastic and even comical.

A frequent indicator of an inexperienced translator is the mixing of registers so that there is a jarring note in a different register in a text which otherwise seems normal. Duff has identified this as one of the features of the "third language" of translators which will be considered in the next lesson. The translator must bear in mind that the register of a text is part of the meaning which must be conveyed across the language gap just as much as the meaning carried by the lexicon and the syntax. There are times when the translator is sorely tempted to "clean up" the text in the process of translation to make it sound more appropriate. There may also be concern that if material is left at a low or inappropriate register the translator will be blamed for "a bad translation." But this type of change can also change the deep meaning, and is an editing function, not a translating one. Englebert[110] cites the case of a legal translator faced with translating several obscene epithets which a woman stated her husband had hurled at her during an altercation; the translator did not wish to offend anyone and substituted much milder terms, and in the process distorted the deeper meaning of the legal document. The guiding principle, if one can put it in a low-register phrase, should be GIGO ("garbage in = garbage out").

Registers can be semantically mapped along a spectrum (Fig. 18-1):

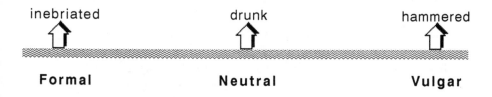

inebriated	drunk	hammered
Formal	**Neutral**	**Vulgar**

**Figure 18-1: Spectrum of Registers
for Concept of "drunk".**

Or the register designation can be combined with other values such as good/bad, pleasant/unpleasant, to produce two-dimensional semantic maps (Figure 18-2):

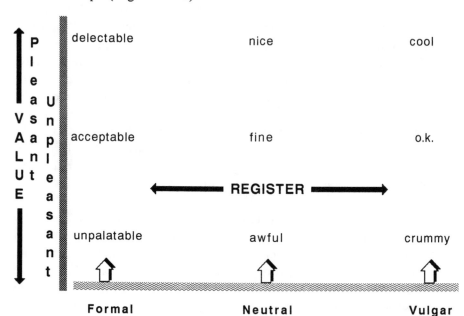

**Figure 18-2: Two-dimensional Semantic Map Showing
Register Spectrum and "unpleasant/pleasant" Value.**

D. TRANSLATION PROBLEMS AND TECHNIQUES.

Phases in the Translation Process.

Translations should not be undertaken in a haphazard fashion, simply "plowing ahead" and working directly from the source text to a final product. A careful and systematic approach will pay considerable dividends in producing a professional and polished translation. What follows has been garnered from the suggestions made by a number of professional translators as well as the author's own experience. Not all of these steps are always possible or applicable, but they represent how a translator should attempt to organize his/her work. (For a systematic approach to poetry translation, see Robert Bly's *The Eight Stages of Translation*).

Phase 1: Preparation. This phase involves deciding just what the translation task involves and who it is for. A quick scan of the material can alert the translator that it is beyond his/her capabilities, or that the time allotted is inadequate. It is also useful to define what type of material is involved: is it literary, technical, descriptive, informational, or communicative? Any special dictionaries, glossaries and other reference material should be requested; it might also be helpful to identify colleagues who might be able to offer assistance. The prime reader should be defined in terms of the register and vocabulary that the TL translation must use. The translator's initial examination of the text may also suggest that a paraphrase or synthesis may be all that is needed, and this should be discussed with the client requesting the translation. Finally, if it seems likely that the material might have been translated previously, it would be worthwhile to check this out, too.

Phase 2: Initial close reading. The text should be read carefully and completely several times to make sure you understand it fully. It is pointless, and professionally damaging, to attempt to translate something if you have problems understanding it in the source language beyond an occasional few words. You should still be able to turn down the job at this point if it is beyond your capabilities and available time. You should also make sure that the copy is completely legible, that no pages are missing, and are numbered to avoid confusion. Ideally, you should have communication with the author or client to clarify any doubts at this stage. Your close reading of the text should include an analysis of the deep meaning and the style involved, to include identifying any idioms, metaphors or literary allusions which you must watch out for.

Phase 3: Research. Unless the text is a very simple one, you may have to do some research before starting the actual translation. This will include reading any relevant background material, checking any unfamiliar words, and finding any available translations of similar material. If the subject is technical, you might want to review some recent publications on similar subjects in both languages, including translations, if at all possible. While you can continue to contact your client (or author), these calls should be kept to a reasonable number to avoid harassment and undermining confidence in your abilities. Saving all the queries for a single call is a good idea.

Phase 4: Rewrite difficult portions (optional). In this phase you might want to re-write (in the source language) any portions of the text you are having trouble with. For example, you might want to re-cast metaphors as similes, or add implicit information which is not needed in the SL but will be in the TL translation. Re-writing is a good way of insuring that you really understand the deep meaning of the SL text.

Phase 5: Translation into a first draft. This is the heart of the process, when the translator takes the SL text, finds the deep meaning, and carries that deep meaning over to the TL. It is important to select "units of meaning" which make sense. These usually are sentences or even complete paragraphs. To translate smaller amounts of text at one time may lead to mistakes. To try and translate all the way through without pause is also dangerous because of the effort involved and the probable decline in efficiency and accuracy. As you translate you should shift back and forth from reading the SL text to writing the TL translation. The actual translation of any "unit of meaning" (sentence or paragraph) should be done quickly, without bothering to polish the TL text at this time. If you do spend too much time on polishing and seeking the best possible phrase, you will lose the continuity of your effort and the train of thought of the deep meaning. You should be striving for a balance of accuracy and proper expression in the target language, while also maintaining a rhythm and pace to your work. Individual rough spots or doubts should be identified so you can go back to them in later drafts (marginal notations are good for this). If you are using a word processor, don't bother cleaning up typographic or spelling errors, since later drafts (or a good spell-check program) will accomplish this. The title of the project should be translated last, when the text is fully understood and translated.

Phase 6: Preparation of the second and subsequent drafts. Unless there is a tight deadline, set aside the initial draft for a few days and then come back to it with a fresh perspective. Go over the draft as if you were the prime reader, looking for rough spots, errors, or anything else which might lead to confusion or mistakes. You should be striving for a reasonable balance between faithfulness to the original (accuracy) and naturalness (style and readability in the TL). Reading the translation aloud or to another person may be helpful. Watch for the information load; is the text too dense and heavy with information, or is it too puffed up and verbose with little meaning? If you have a willing colleague, have him/her look at both the SL original and your TL translation.

Phase 7: Editing and final draft. Here you should be alert to format, margins, punctuation, spelling, grammar, and all those other factors which go into making a decent final text. If the translation is for internal or informal use, you might want to include a "translator's note" to indicate a problem or to clarify a possibly ambiguous point. If the translation is for publication, these notes should be avoided if at all possible through additional research and consultation with other translators. Translations for publication frequently are done in "camera ready" form, with no typographic errors or other irregularities, so that they can be photographed or photocopied for direct use in a publication.

Phase 8: Final check. Before turning in the finished product you should look it over one last time to be sure that nothing has been left out, and that no errors were introduced in the editing stage. The document may require some form of certification, notarization or legalization; a common form uses the phrase "I certify that this translation was done to the best of my ability." Keep a copy of the translation for your own protection should it get lost or be challenged, and also to build up a file of work you can show future clients. If the material is confidential or unpublished, you may need to delete certain names and other data to protect your client.

E. COGNATES.
fc = false cognate   pc = partial cognate (be careful)
pfc = partial false cognate (be very careful)

PARIENTES (fc) = relatives.
≠ parents; instead use "padres."
PARTICIPAR (pfc) = to be involved in something.
Can also = to share something like news or an invitation.
PARTICULAR (fc) ≠ demanding; instead use "exigente."
= private: "es un automóvil particular."
PERFECCIONAR (pfc) = to make perfect.
Usually means to improve or increase one's professional qualifications or training: "Perfeccionó su inglés."
PERSONERO (fc) ≠ person; instead use "persona."
= spokesperson, mouthpiece:
"el personero (or "portavoz") de la Casa Blanca."
PERSPECTIVA (pfc) = perspective in drawing and architecture.
Also = viewpoint, prospects for the future.
PETULANCIA (fc) ≠ petulance in sense of irritable, impatient.
= insolence, vanity.
PLANTEAR (fc) ≠ plant.
= to raise an issue, pose a problem, theorize, postulate.

F. PROVERBS AND IDIOMS.
Ni a tiros   Not for anything.
Ni mucho menos   Far from it.
No cabe duda   There is no doubt.
No darse por entendido   To pretend not to understand.
No dejar piedra por mover   To leave no stone unturned.
No es oro todo lo que reluce.   All that glitters is not gold.

No es tan fiero el león como lo pintan.
   His bark is worse than his bite.
No hay de qué   Don't mention it.
No hay mal que por bien no venga.   Every cloud has a silver lining.
No me importa un comino   I don't give a damn.

Figure 18-3. "You must be the bilingual interpreter."

LESSON 19

A. HISTORY OF TRANSLATION.

The Impact of Linguistics and Communications Theory.

Contemporary approaches to translation and interpretation have been profoundly influenced by the science of linguistics, and by communications theory. Earlier approaches to translation (up to the first few decades of the 20th Century) had been firmly grounded in a pragmatic view with little, if any, theoretical foundation. What theory existed consisted of somewhat arbitrary "rules" for translation, and the offerings of literature or philology.

The contributions made by early 20th Century linguists, especially those of the structural field, have increasingly suggested the emergence of a linguistic science which can make meaningful theoretical contributions to translation. The work of Ferdinand de Saussure, the Linguistic Circles of Copenhagen and Prague, and a number of American linguists have steadily strengthened the argument that the theoretical foundations for translation as a science can be found. The associated sciences of semantics, semiotics and anthropology have further buttressed their position. In particular, the scientific linking of language and culture has permitted the anthropologist to suggest helpful approaches to the translator/interpreter. As a result, a number of writings in recent years have argued for systematic analysis of the field of "translation studies," or "translatology."[111]

The field of communications has also weighed in, arguing that language can be discussed in terms of communications concepts such as transmitters, receivers, channels, information load, redundancy, and noise. This focus has an obvious lead-in to computer applications, and to the dream of machine translation (or at least machine-aided translation), using advanced computers. The debate on translation thus has come to be framed in terms of whether it is an art (the esthetic approach), a craft (the pragmatic), or a science (the linguistic/communications approach). Extreme positions are held in all three of these possibilities, although many also argue that translation is in fact all three, and the emphasis on art, craft or science depends on the particular type of material being translated, the personal approach of the translator, and the needs of the prime reader who will receive the end product.

Perhaps the appropriate parallel to the relationship between linguistic theory and translation is that of physics and engineering, or mechanics and architecture. The practitioner ignores theory at his or her peril, but the theoretical and scientific foundation alone cannot a good translation make. Or, in the words of Octavio Paz: "No hay ni puede haber una ciencia de la traducción, aunque ésta puede y debe estudiarse científicamente."[112]

The 20th Century emphasis on a linguistic science as a foundation for translation has also led to a greater separation between the study of translation and that of interpretation. Increasingly there has been an awareness that the mechanism by which the brain processes written versus spoken language is different, and that the "switching mechanism" which allows transference from one language to another is not the same for the written word as the spoken. This has fundamental implications for the teaching of translation versus interpretation, since one of the apparent findings is that to be a successful interpreter one must have the interpreting "switching mechanism" developed at a very early age, generally through the process of growing up exposed to two languages. If this switching mechanism for interpretation is not so developed, it is very difficult to acquire as an adolescent or adult. The conclusion may well be that it is extremely difficult, if not impossible, to teach simultaneous interpretation to someone without this switching mechanism in place. Successful translation teaching, on the other hand, relies on being able first to express oneself effectively in one's own ("target") language, and then acquiring the written forms (grammatical, lexical, semantic and stylistic) of any number of second ("source") languages. This process is clearly possible, and indeed forms the basis for the teaching of both foreign languages, and of translation itself.

B. TRANSLATION TIDBIT.
Two hotel signs:[113]
"Visit our restaurant, where you can eat Middle East foods in an European ambulance."
"The water in this hotel is safe to drink. It has been passed by the manager."

C. THEORY OF TRANSLATION.

The "Third Language."

Alan Duff, in his book *The Third Language*,[114] lays out an interesting idea which has value for both the theory and practice of translation. He begins by noting that a great deal of the translated material he encounters does not sound quite natural, and he suggests that the basic reason is that all too many translators write in a "third language" that is somewhere between the source language and the target language. Although the problem is one which mainly affects translators working *out of* their native tongue, Duff argues that the phenomenon is also observable in translators writing into their mother tongue, so that the explanation goes deeper than a simple inability to write clearly in the target language.

It is easy enough to remember any number of blatant examples of bad translations which may use the words of the target language, but are written by someone who is not familiar enough with the TL to sound natural. Duff's examples reveal that many native speakers writing in their mother tongue are somehow unable to break totally away from the words, syntax and style of the SL, and thus sound unnatural in the TL. (For the sake of simplicity Duff uses only examples of translations into English, but his basic arguments are valid in other languages as well). The problem is, in part, one of inappropriate choices of the words, although it also includes the way words are put together (syntax and style). The problem, he notes, goes beyond the dictionaries, for "the dictionary is concerned with words, not with *how the words are put together*." (His emphasis). In a typical "third language" translation the words are all in English, there are no spelling or grammatical mistakes, but it still "sounds foreign" because of the way the words are put together in the sentence or because they are combined in unfamiliar or odd ways. Here is an example Duff gives of a set of instructions for a Japanese power tool:

"General Operational Precautions
5. Do not put the power tool and accessories in work beyond their abilities.
6. Keep unauthorized people, especially children away from the power tool."

Why does this read like a translation and not natural English? Some of the features which place it in Duff's "third language" would include:
-one does not speak of "putting a tool in work"
-a tool does not have "ability"
-the word "unauthorized" is inappropriate in a home situation, which is where the power tool was designed to be used.

How can we move this example from its "third language" into English? Here is a possible solution:
5. Do not overload the power tool.
6. Keep the power tool away from children and anyone not familiar with how to operate it.

In his book Duff examines the "third language" in three categories: lexical problems, structural problems, and finally difficulties with style and transference from one culture to another. To pick up one single aspect of his first category, we note how a mix of registers can make the sentence sound unnatural. Here are some examples he cites:
"The architects and engineers had quite a lot of trouble with these columns before the desired optical effect was achieved. The thing was, that in spite of the raised pattern the concrete rods could be seen through the glass." The over-all register of this passage is generally formal and technical; it is a description of an aspect of architecture or building construction. But there are two jarring notes, two short clauses which are in a lower register (colloquial or chatty): "quite a lot" and "the thing was."

Another example is from a Brazilian trade advertisement in a British newspaper: "But at present, iron ore, manganese, maize, tool machinery, male and female and children's fashion products, shoes, cars and lorries, airplanes and ships are components of Brazilian exports." Here the over-all register of a commercial advertisement contains some inappropriate words: "male and female" (more appropriate to an anthropological report) and "component" (more suited to a scientific study). A more balanced register would perhaps begin with "Brazilian exports include ..." and speak of "clothing for men, women and children."

The mixing of metaphors also creates this sense of "third language": "the situation opened a wedge between the intellectuals and the masses - a wound that, in the case of Argentina at least, healed poorly and late." In terms of the analysis of metaphors in Lesson 17, the basic element being described is the gap between the intellectuals and the masses. But two metaphors are used (and mixed) to characterize that gap: first that of a wedge being driven between them, and second that of a wound.

Application: Duff provides a fresh look at the recurring problem of translations that seem adequate, but do not "sound" natural. His concept that this is due to a "third language" is a useful one that should lead us to examine our own translations to see if this indeed is the language we are using as our TL.

D. TRANSLATION PROBLEMS AND TECHNIQUES.

Numbers and Measurements.

The Spanish-English translator will find a few idiosyncrasies in numbers and measurements which may cause problems.

Numbers. The English usage regarding commas and periods to indicate decimals and to separate three-digit clusters in large numbers is exactly reversed in most Spanish-speaking countries:
English: pi= 3.1416;   1,235,600 inhabitants
Spanish: pi= 3,1416;   1.235.600 habitantes.

There is also a problem with the idea of "billion" in the U.S., where "billion" means "a thousand million": 1,000,000,000. But in Latin America, Europe and much of the rest of the world, "billion" means "a million million": 1,000,000,000,000. The correct translation of the U.S. "billion" into Spanish usage would be "mil milliones," and the correct translation from Spanish "billion" to English would be "trillion."

Amount	English	Spanish
1,000,000	million	millón
1,000,000,000	billion	mil millones
1,000,000,000,000	trillion	billón

In manuscript (handwritten) Spanish and English there is possible confusion between the "1" and the "7." A U.S. English 7 may be confused with the Spanish 1 because both are written the same way. Spanish avoids the confusion by crossing the 7, but this usage is not common in the U.S. Fortunately, most translators work from typed texts, especially when dealing with figures, and in typed texts the numbers are identical in both languages.

Measurements. The United States is one of the very few countries in the world which has resisted conversion to the metric system, and this can cause translation difficulties. When the use of a unit of measure is symbolic, and is not intended to be precise, the translation should be into the unit of measure best known to the prime reader, with no attempt at precision:
"he was miles from home" = "estaba a kilómetros de su hogar"
"he drank many quarts of wine" = "tomó muchos litros de vino".

However, in many other cases, especially in commercial, technical and legal translation, the intent is to give a much more precise measurement, and here the translator has a dilemma. If s/he leaves the measurement in the original SL unit, it may seem strange and incomprehensible to the TL prime reader. On the other hand, a precise mathematical conversion may also sound strange, and may convey an image of precision which the SL writer never intended. The translator should be guided by the intent of the SL writer and the needs of the TL prime reader, but these two factors may also be hard

to determine. In the final analysis, it is usually the translator's personal and professional decision, based on the best information available. The following example will illustrate the problem.
Original English: "He was two inches short of the goal."
Translation, no conversion: "Le faltaban dos pulgadas para la meta."
Imprecise translation: "Le faltaban cinco centímetros para la meta."
Precise translation: "Le faltaban 5,08 centímetros para la meta."

Monetary units also pose difficulties, especially when it is not clear if the sign "$" means "dollars," "pesos," or some other currency. When there is a possibility of confusion the considerate source language writer will specify, using any one of a number of standard notations, such as US$, or the abbreviation "mn" ("moneda nacional" meaning legal tender of the country involved). The U.S. dollar is frequently taken as a standard due to the relatively low inflation rate of this currency, but the dollar also changes in value over time. The translator should avoid making any conversion from one currency to another because of the great fluctuations in conversion rates over the years.

E. COGNATES.
fc = false cognate   pc = partial cognate (be careful)
pfc = partial false cognate (be very careful)

POLITICA (pfc) = politics or policy (in a political sense).
    ≠ policy in the insurance sense;
    instead use "póliza de seguros."
POPULACION (fc) ≠ population;
    instead use "población" or "pueblo."
    = the act of populating an empty region.
POSICION (pfc) = generally refers to physical position.
    ≠ viewpoint or argument; instead use "punto de vista."
PRECIOSO (pfc) = of great value.
    Also = beautiful: "María es una niña preciosa."
PRECISO (pfc) = exact.
    Also = necessary: "es preciso hacerlo ahora."
PRESUMIR (fc) = to boast or brag.
    ≠ suppose; instead use "suponer": "supongo que estará aquí."

PRETENDER (fc) = to attempt or try: "pretende ser jefe."
≠ simulate or assume an identity falsely;
instead use "simular" or "fingir."
PRIVADO (pfc) = narrower meaning than in English, and usually is
restricted to mean "personal": "carta privada."
PROCURAR (pfc) = to obtain.
Also usually = to attempt or try.

F. PROVERBS AND IDIOMS.

No me importa un pito   I could care less.
No se ganó Zamora en una hora.   Rome wasn't built in an hour.
No tener remedio   To be beyond help.
No vale un comino   Not worth anything.
Obra empezada, medio acabada.   The hardest part is the beginning.
Obrar en poder de   In the hands of.
Padre mercader, hijo caballero, nieto limosnero.
        Shirtsleeves to shirtsleeves in three generations.
Pagar a plazos   Payment on the installment plan.
Pagar en la misma moneda   To get even.
Palabra   Word of honor.
Para colmo de males   The last straw.

LESSON 20

A. HISTORY OF TRANSLATION.

History of Modern Conference Interpretation.

The division between translation and interpretation was boosted by the growth in conference interpretation in the 20th Century. Prior to this growth the need for interpretation at international conferences was limited by several factors. For one, the number of such conferences was much more limited in the past due to the less intensive level of international relations as well as logistical problems such as transportation. But more importantly, up until the 20th Century diplomacy was generally conducted in a single language. In the period of the great empires the language would be that of the imperial power. Thus, under the Romans every citizen involved in trade or political relations with Rome was assumed to have a working knowledge of Latin, and there was no need for interpretation. Through the Middle Ages Latin continued as the language of the educated European person, to be replaced by French in the 17th Century. From the Treaty of Westphalia (1648) until World War I French was the dominant language of diplomacy, and thus there continued to be no need for conference interpretation. If special circumstances arose where a particular individual at an international meeting could not speak the dominant language of diplomacy, there was always the device of "chuchotage" (French for "whispering") to accommodate him or her. In this procedure the interpreter would sit behind and to one side of the principal and whisper a running interpretation (sometimes highly condensed) of the proceedings. This procedure is still used today where technical facilities are limited, or where heads of state meet on a one-on-one and face-to-face basis.

But the 20th Century brought a much more complex set of international arrangements, with many more actors less disposed (for political and nationalistic reasons) to accept any one language as the dominant one. Furthermore, the number and subject of international conferences has grown explosively, with many technical ones which require specialized vocabulary, jargon, and knowledge. The first signs of significant change came with the Versailles Peace Conference in 1919 at the end of World War I. The French felt theirs should be the sole working language, but U.S. President Woodrow Wilson and British Prime Minister Lloyd George (neither of whom spoke French) argued that English should also be used, since the English-speaking world was now larger than the French. The French resisted, presenting counter-arguments that Italian should also be a working language (but with French as the authoritative). In the end both French and English were accepted as equally authoritative, and with this decision some 200 years of French domination of the language of diplomacy came to an end.[115] The mechanics of interpretation at the 1919 Conference were handled by a small staff of consecutive interpreters, aided by a larger group of bilingual and trilingual secretaries to assist with the drafting of written documents.

The Post-World War I League of Nations also used consecutive interpretation, although the process was becoming increasingly unwieldy due to the number of languages involved and the technical nature of much of the material. There was also much debate over whether the "short" or "long" form of consecutive interpretation was better. Those advocating the "short" form argued that the interpreter should interpret one sentence at a time in order to minimize the possibility of error. The supporters of the long form held that much meaning and continuity was lost this way, and that it was better to have the interpreter come in at infrequent intervals. In its extreme version this meant that the speaker would give his/her whole speech uninterrupted, while the interpreter took notes and then would speak at the end and give the speech all over again in the second language. When this occurred there was increasing pressure for the interpreter to compress the speech and simply give a summary of it in order to save time. This would sometimes create strained situations when a very short summary by an interpreter would reveal that much of the original speech was irrelevant fluff. There was also the opposite case when the interpreter's version might be far more flowery and eloquent than the original. It was very tempting for an intelligent, eloquent and frustrated interpreter to improve on the original speech, and some did.

The technology of the telephone made a key breakthrough between the Wars when the International Business Machine Company proposed to the League of Nations that its newly developed system of microphones, wires, switching mechanism and listening headsets be used for simultaneous interpretation. This could now be accomplished in such a way that the interpreters could work into the second language as the speaker spoke in the first, with their interpreted words reaching the other delegates through the microphone-wire-switchboard-headset system. In theory, the simultaneous system could work into any number of languages at the same time, depending on the availability of interpreters and the switching capacity of the telephone system. Such an arrangement was used on a limited basis by the League and several of its subordinate organs in the 1930's. The first major use of the IBM system, and thus the first real test of simultaneous interpretation, was at the Nazi War Crimes Trial of the International Military Tribunal in Nuremberg, Germany after World War II. The IBM equipment was now twenty years old, aging, and very cumbersome. Further, the trials were complex, long, and covered a wide range of subject matter. But with some improvisation, both the equipment and the interpreters stood up well and simultaneous interpretation became the distinctive feature of international meetings.

And so it was natural that the newly formed United Nations Secretariat would adopt the simultaneous approach, using some of the same interpreters who had worked at Nuremberg. There was opposition by some of the older interpreters (and diplomats) whose experience was exclusively in consecutive. They argued that consecutive was more accurate than simultaneous, but as simultaneous interpreters grew in number and practice this was proven not to be necessarily so, and in any case the tremendous saving in time brought by simultaneous made it worth the possible marginal drop in accuracy. The issue of official working languages at the United Nations was also contentious. It was clear from the start that it would be impossible to have simultaneous into all the languages of the member states, so some choices had to be made. The preliminary San Francisco UN conference had shown how using multiple languages in translation increased the paper output geometrically; the San Francisco Conference published all written documents in five "official" languages (English, French, Russian, Chinese and Spanish), and ended up with 78 tons of paper, or an average daily output of a half a million sheets.[116] Upon starting their operations in the New York Headquarters, the Secretariat was able to initially keep the "working" languages down to two (English and French) although the Spanish-speaking nations, who then represented about 1/3 of the voting strength of the UN, were later successful in their efforts to add Spanish as a third UN working language. In the Organization of American States the problem is ameliorated by having only two "working" languages (Spanish and English), while there are four "official" languages (Spanish, English, Portuguese and French). The Surinamese have not insisted on adding Dutch.

B. TRANSLATION TIDBIT.
Two translations[117] from the magazine of Iberia Airlines (Spain):
   "El Corte Inglés disposes of 16 stores all over Spain. They are devoted to Fashion and its accessories, to the Home, to the Decoration, to the Sports..."
   A U.S. airline flying to Brazil advertised luxury "rendezvous lounges" on its jets, but discovered that in Portuguese the term meant a room hired on a short-term basis for love-making.

C. THEORY OF TRANSLATION.

Theory of Interpretation.

   It is generally accepted that translation refers to the written word, while interpretation implies working with the spoken. Even though these two skills are quite different, there is a relationship between them, and interpretation can provide some useful exercises in the process of improving one's translation skills as well as advancing in the study of a language generally.

Interpretation includes:

Escort interpretation, in which the interpreter accompanies an individual or small group of individuals, usually foreign visitors, and acts as a go-between in their contacts with the host country. The interpreter not only facilitates conversations between the visitors and the natives of the host country, but also frequently serves as a guide in explaining local sights and customs. In these types of situations the interpreter has considerable flexibility, and exercises much initiative and creativity.

Consecutive interpretation, where the interpreter renders short portions of the speaker's utterances when the speaker pauses. These portions are usually sentences, but sometimes can be paragraphs or longer portions. Consecutive interpretation is frequently used for official meetings, and has the distinct disadvantage of requiring at least twice as much time as the straightforward presentation of a speech or remarks. (In some diplomatic situations this is in fact an advantage, since it gives the speakers time to think through their remarks or reaction). For the interpreter, consecutive requires close attention, an excellent memory, the ability to take good rapid notes, and a willingness to submerge any personal opinion regarding the subject at hand.

Simultaneous or conference interpretation, which is the most demanding of all the categories, since the interpreter must speak in the target language at the same time as s/he hears the original words in the source language. Usually this is accomplished with the help of electronic equipment, and the interpreter sits in a sound-proof booth hearing the original words through headphones while speaking the source language words into a microphone. In the "chuchotage" variant of simultaneous interpretation, the interpreter sits close to the recipient of the interpretation and whispers the target language interpretation in her/his ear.

Oral interpretation can make several contributions to the study and practice of written translation. The "chuchotage" method is a good way to involve a whole roomful of foreign language students in an active exercise; the instructor pairs off groups of students and has one in each pair whisper consecutive or simultaneous interpretation while a student or the instructor delivers a talk to the class as a whole. A further exercise involves sight translation, which is somewhere in between written translation and oral interpretation. In a typical classroom exercise, the instructor projects a paragraph on the screen using a Vu-graph. Selected students then take the paragraph and, without the benefit of dictionary or consultations, render it verbally and directly into the target language. Although the end product tends to be somewhat ragged, it is a good vehicle for developing speed and allows a general class critique of the student's performance. An alternate procedure would be to combine the paired-off "chuchotage" approach with the projected sight translation.

Interpretation, like translation, is communication, albeit under very special circumstances. The interpreter receives an oral message in the SL, analyzes it, processes it into the TL, and transmits it orally to a receiver. The special circumstances involve the need for speed without sacrificing accuracy, and hopefully not sacrificing style or elegance either. The interpreter has an additional problem not faced by the translator of the written word; oral speech is usually accompanied by non-verbal messages such as tone, pitch, loudness, body language, gestures, etc. How is the interpreter to deal with these elements, which also convey meaning?

Seleskovich[118] describes the interpretation process as follows:
1. Auditory perceptions of a linguistic utterance which carries meaning. Apprehension of the language and comprehension of the message through a process of analysis and exegesis.
2. Immediate and deliberate discarding of the wording and retention of the mental representation of the message (concepts, ideas, etc).
3. Production of a new utterance in the target language which must meet a dual requirement; it must express the original message in its entirety, and it must be geared to the recipient.

Note how step 2 and the second part of step 1 are the analogy to the translator's procedure of stripping the SL of its surface structure (i.e., word and syntax), and dealing with the deep meaning. In simultaneous interpretation all three steps are occurring at the same time, which is an astonishing demand to make on the human brain. Those who have never done simultaneous interpretation find it difficult to believe that a person can speak in one language at the same time as s/he is also listening in another. But the other step (i.e., stripping the words down to their deep meaning and transferring them to the TL) is equally demanding. Perhaps what makes it all possible is the built-in redundancy in human language (as much as 50%), plus the reinforcement through non-verbal communication, which allows the interpreter some room for maneuver.

Interpreters are fond of quoting the Latin saying, "scripta manet -- verba volant" (written words remain for ever, but the spoken word flies away or vanishes). However, what vanishes is the surface structure of the spoken word, and the deep meaning should remain in the brain of the receiver in the TL. Interestingly enough, many simultaneous interpreters will say that they have trouble remembering the details of what they interpreted, especially after a long and arduous session; it is as though the brain deliberately "dumps" its memory like a computer to avoid overloading.

Just as the translator commits a basic error if s/he tries to translate word-for-word, so does the interpreter. Although it is possible to stick close to a word-for-word interpretation in very similar languages with similar structures (i.e. Spanish and Portuguese), the error can be blatant when they are different, as is the case with Spanish and English. To give one example, English tends to put the noun at the end of a string of adjectives, while in Spanish the reverse is true. How then would we interpret the following phrase word for word (and simultaneously, without waiting for the noun at the end): "the good, happy, eager, noble and ever-present man"

D. TRANSLATION PROBLEMS AND TECHNIQUES.

<u>Interpretation.</u>

This section will address some practical aspects of escort and consecutive interpretation because of the probability that as an advanced student of Spanish you will sometime in your career be asked to serve as an interpreter of this type. Please note that we are

not talking about simultaneous or conference interpreting. This type of interpretation requires highly developed language skills and an extensive period of training. Even then, only a small number of people who speak two or more languages well can really call themselves qualified simultaneous interpreters. You should never accept an assignment as a simultaneous interpreter without this preparation.

On the other hand, if you pursue a career in international business or diplomacy, or travel extensively abroad, or have many contacts with people who speak other tongues, there is a very good chance that you will at some point be asked to serve as an escort or consecutive interpreter. This section is designed to provide you with some warnings and techniques which may help you if this ever happens. If the nature of your career puts you into a situation where languages are important, your peers and supervisors will probably know of your language abilities (indeed, you should tell them). If you are identified as a person with some language skill, the day may come when you will be called on to accompany a foreign visitor, or act as interpreter for that visitor to your office or company. Your boss may not want to hire a professional interpreter, and you will be presented with an opportunity to show your worth to the company; on the other hand, if your actual language abilities are not as great as you (or your boss) think, you may also be handed an opportunity to embarrass yourself and your company. But the chances are that the opportunity will come, and you should do what you can to prepare for it. If you are interested in knowing more about the very demanding field of simultaneous interpretation, consult the book by Danika Seleskovich. For an account of a U.S. interpreter in the psychologically difficult situation of interpreting in a hostile environment at a truce conference, see the book by Robert Ekvall.[119]

The U.S. State Department takes the approach mentioned above, namely that a professional Foreign Service officer who has received language training may well be called on to do escort or consecutive interpretation in his/her career because there may not be the time, money or opportunity available to get a professional interpreter. The Department's Office of Language Services has prepared a "Checklist for Nonprofessional Interpreters" from which we have adapted the following suggestions for someone who might be called on unexpectedly to serve this function.[120]

Pre-meeting preparations.
1. Do not agree to act as an interpreter until you know just what the meeting is about (you should be familiar with the subject matter and the participants). Find out in what direction you are being asked to interpret (just into English, which would be the easier task, or also into Spanish). Make sure everyone knows you are not a professional interpreter, and that you will not be expected to do simultaneous.

2. Research as much as you can about the meeting. Read background materials and minutes or records of prior meetings. Make a bilingual glossary of any acronyms and technical terms you are likely to encounter.

3. Check the physical arrangements for the meeting. You should sit or stand next to your principal if you are interpreting for just one person. If you are interpreting between two principals, you should be between the two.

4. Find out ahead of time how many people you will be expected to interpret for. Even though only the principal may be mentioned, it is possible that s/he is accompanied by assistants who will also need help.

5. Talk to your principal ahead of time to see how s/he wants to proceed. Make suggestions according to your choice (do you want him/her to pause after each sentence, paragraph, or complete speech or statement).

6. Take a suitable note pad and at least two writing instruments. If the event is a sit-down meeting, a large or legal-side pad is fine, but if the event is a formal dinner or speech, your pad should be no larger than 3x5 inches to avoid awkward situations and to keep from ruining a possible "photo opportunity."

During the meeting.
7. You must sit or stand where you can hear the speaker. Don't be shy about moving if you have to. Speak clearly and with self-confidence, but not so loud as to distract those who are not making use of your services.

8. Use the first person. Say: "I accept your proposal," not "the Ambassador accepts your proposal."

9. Avoid giving your personal opinion; you are there as a faithful mirror of the speaker, not as a negotiator or editorial commentator. Avoid saying things like "he says yes but probably means maybe," or "he is lying like a dog."

10. Move through the preliminaries and social niceties at a fast (but not rude) clip, and slow down and be redundant if necessary during key points in the meeting.

11. If the speaker goes too long without giving you the opportunity to interpret, gently remind him that your capabilities are limited and you need to have the speech in shorter bursts. This may be hard to do in formal occasions, but you must do it if you are to be effective.

12. During social events and walk-around situations, keep your principal in sight and don't get carried away with your own socializing. Your principal should be able to get you in 5 seconds if s/he needs you.

13. Pace yourself; don't burn out in 10 minutes since you might have to keep going for a couple of hours.

14. Toasts are tricky. Get the text ahead of time if at all possible and work out a written translation (with professional help if you can). When you deliver the toast, try to project the same emotional tone that your principal does.

An important aspect not mentioned in the State Department's checklist is the use of notes. You should not try and write everything down, nor attempt to use shorthand, since there will probably be too much information to handle. Instead, jot down a few key ideas, and any important numbers or proper names (these usually give the most trouble). Your notes should be in the target language, so that as you listen in the source language you will already be formulating in your own mind what you will be saying in the target language. You can practice these skills on a frequent basis listening to oral material in the source language, writing notes in the target language, and then doing a consecutive delivery to someone who knows both languages.

E. COGNATES.

fc = false cognate   pc = partial cognate (be careful)
pfc = partial false cognate (be very careful)

PROMOCION (fc) ≠ promotion in sense of advancement;
    instead use "ascenso."
    = a sale in a store or the promotion of a new product.
    Also can mean a class in a school: "la promoción de 1989."
PROPAGANDA (pfc) = political or ideological propaganda.
    Also = advertising.
QUITAR (fc) ≠ quit; instead use "abandonar," "terminar" or "salir."
    = remove.
RADICAR (fc) = to live or settle somewhere.
    ≠ radical.
RAZONADO (pfc) = reasoned.
    When used with a list, plan, drawing or catalog, means
    "commented" or "annotated."
REALIZAR (fc) ≠ realize in sense of being aware;
    instead use "darse cuenta."
    = to accomplish or achieve something: "realicé mi propósito."
RECORDAR (fc) ≠ record; instead use "grabar" or "registrar."
    = remember.
REFRIGERIO (fc) ≠ refrigerator; instead use "nevera" or "heladera."
    = snack or light meal.

F. PROVERBS AND IDIOMS.

Parece mentira   It seems impossible.
Pares y nones   Odds and evens.
Pasado de moda   Out of style.
Pedir prestado   To borrow.
Perro que ladra no muerde.   A barking dog doesn't bite.
Plan de estudios   Curriculum; course of study.
Poderoso caballero es don dinero.   Money talks.
Poner el grito en el cielo   To raise hell; make a fuss.
Poner en claro   To clear up.
Poner en marcha   To put into motion; to start.

Figure 20-1. Machine translation.

LESSON 21

A. HISTORY OF TRANSLATION.

<u>Court Interpretation in the US.</u>

One specialized field of interpretation involves assisting defendants in the U.S. court system who do not speak English. In recent years this problem has grown increasingly serious in the United States because of the large numbers such cases, and the impact of the Federal Court Interpreter's Act. The basic principle is that equal justice under the law cannot be guaranteed unless the defendant fully understands the language being used in his or her case. However, different standards and the lack of qualified interpreters meant that in practice few non-English speaking defendants were really provided with this guarantee.

The 1978 Federal Court Interpreter's Act was an important milestone not just for the legal system, but also because it was the first (and so far the only) government attempt to regulate and certify the qualifications of interpreters and translators. Unlike many other countries, in the United States anyone can call themselves an interpreter or translator without any check on their qualifications. The 1978 Act was designed to bring some order to this situation, as far as the Federal Courts were concerned. The Act was introduced in 1977 by the Senate's Judicial Improvement Committee, which singled out "citizens of Spanish, Puerto Rican, Chinese, native American and other heritages, as well as deaf citizens who must communicate in sign language."[121]

In order to set a standard for court interpreters an exam was prepared, with Spanish as the test case. The exam was supervised by the Office of Court Reporting and Interpreting Services of the Administrative Office of the United States Courts in Washington.[122] The first part of the test is a preliminary screening exam to see if the candidate has the approximately two years of college (in both languages) which was deemed to be the minimum level to understand legal proceedings in Federal courts. Those passing the screening test are then subjected to an oral test in which they are required to interpret a series of simulated courtroom situations such as arguments before a jury by a defense attorney, cross-examination, the judge's instructions to a jury, and other realistic scenarios. The pass rate for this rigorous exam has been running at only about 5-7%, and as a result the number of Federally-certified court interpreters falls far short of the requirements. The result is that defendants are frequently deprived of their right to a legal proceeding they can understand. Stop-gap measures have included bringing in semi-qualified individuals or family members, but these frequently cause difficulties by their incompetence or by becoming personally involved in the proceedings and giving their own versions of events.

Court interpreting has special challenges. It usually is consecutive, and the interpreter has to work in both directions. If an interpreter is working alone, s/he is repeating everything that is said in the proceedings, and thus speaks as much as everyone else put together. A particularly difficult problem for the court interpreter is that of the level, or "register" of the language being used. The defendant is frequently a person with a relatively low level of education, who may even be illiterate and use slang or jargon unfamiliar to the interpreter. The interpreter must also deal with the legal jargon and the language of the average member of the jury (if one is involved). If the interpreter takes the defendant's words spoken at a low register and presents them to the judge and jury at a much higher level, then there is a distortion which can create a dangerous misconception of the defendant's thoughts and actions in the case. It is said that doctors bury their mistakes. Among court interpreters there is a saying that they either send their mistakes to jail or let them out on the street to commit additional crimes.

B. TRANSLATION TIDBIT.
Sign at a restaurant in Albuquerque, New Mexico: "Our Nachos are the Tostada Town."
Some brand names cause problems in Spanish: Herculon carpets (stress the last two syllables). Robo carwashes. The "Nova" automobile. [123]

C. THEORY OF TRANSLATION.

Special Problems of Translating Poetry and Dramatic Works.

The translation of poetry and dramatic works for the theater are subfields within the already specialized field of literary translation. They deserve consideration, because more has been written about translating these two categories (especially poetry) than any other field of translation. There is also the continuing debate over whether or not these two forms of literary expression can in fact be translated at all. The basic problem with translating poetry is that we are really dealing with double translation, since poetry, in whatever language, has a sub-language of its own. Thus, when dealing with poetry translation, we must modify our Nida-Larson diagram of Lesson 3 as follows (Figure 21-1): we go from poetry in the source language (Poem SL) to the deep meaning of the poem (DM). We then transfer the deep meaning to the target language's prose (Prose TL) and then make a second translation from that to a poem in the target language (Poem TL).

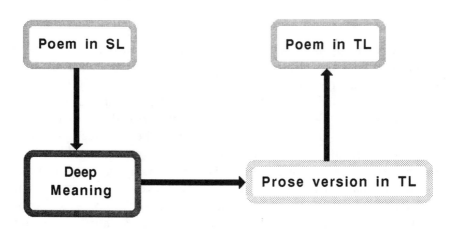

Figure 21-1: Poetry translation

It could be argued that it is possible to go directly from deep meaning to the poem in the target language, but it seems unlikely that a poetry translator could do this without the intermediate step of mulling over (at least in his/her mind) what the deep meaning was in target language prose. One immediate implication of this scheme is that to translate poetry into poetry you must be a poet as well as a translator. There is simply no way to get around this, since if the translator is to produce something in the language of poetry in the target language, s/he must be able to write poetry in that language. This immediately narrows the field of available human beings considerably; how many translators are also able poets, and how many of these are willing to translate poetry instead of creating their own poems?

If one is content to leave the translation at its next to last stage (i.e., in target language prose), then the translator does not have to be a poet. All that is required is that s/he be able to understand the poem in the SL, extract the deep meaning, and then restructure that deep meaning in the prose of the TL. But what comes out is not poetry, and clearly much is lost. What is lost are those things which make poetry so fascinating: rhythm, meter, rhyme, onomatopoeia, and the physical structure of the words of the poem on the printed page.

Another approach would be to acknowledge that in translating poetry there are inevitable trade-offs; one can emphasize the deep meaning, or the rhythm, or the physical structure, or the rhyming verse, but probably can never carry all of these from SL to TL in a satisfactory way. Some poetry translations will thus appeal more from the esthetic perspective, others from the intellectual, others from the sense of understanding the deep meaning, and others as demonstrations of technical expertise in translation. But it seems impossible that a translator/poet could achieve all of these in one version. For a demonstration of this, it is useful to compare various translations of the same poem by several authors. Bassnett-McGuire[124] gives a good example when she takes Catullus' Poem 13 (describing a humorous invitation to dinner) and compares translations into English made in several different centuries.

It is quite possible, of course, for the translated poem to be superior in some ways to the original. Fitts, for example[125] argues that Edgar Alan Poe's "The Raven" sounds better in Spanish poetry translation than in Poe's own English original because of the heightened dramatic powers of that language. Fitts also takes a famous poem in Spanish (González Martínez' call to twist the Modernist swan's neck) and its translation into English by John Peale Bishop, and notes how the Spanish language can achieve its purpose with more abstract ideas, while English demands a more concrete and specific description.[126] For the student interested in the special problems of translating poetry from Spanish into English, the prefaces written by translators in presenting their work are valuable sources. Those of Walter Owen have been noted in Lesson 17; Felstiner's reflections on his translations of Pablo Neruda are also revealing.[127]

The issue of translatability or untranslatability of poetry remains unresolved and open-ended. Perhaps the most useful comment in this connection was made by García Yebra, who stated that a good prose translation in prose is better than a bad translation in verse; but a good translation in verse is better than a good translation in prose.[128] We are left with the perennial problem of what a "good translation" is, and how to achieve it through what combination of tradeoffs. As with so many other aspects of translation, there is no easy answer. Perfection may be impossible to achieve, but it is indeed essential that we make the attempt.

Also of value is the diagram used by Holmes to indicate the range of possibilities in translating poetry which summarizes some of the trade-offs described above. In an extensive commentary,[129] Holmes describes the different possibilities in this arrangement (see Figure 21-2). Verse translation of the poem lies at the overlap of the various forms of poetry and the various forms of interpretation derived from the original poem. Other forms of interpretation range from verse translation to various prose essays about the poem; other forms of poetry range from imitation to a poem only very loosely connected to the original poem through its inspirational force.

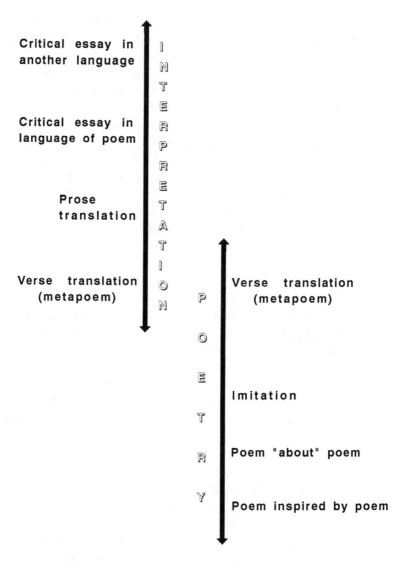

Figure 21-2: Holmes' model of poetry translation

The problem of translating dramatic works for the theater has many of the same features as poetry, with some additional ones imposed by the idiosyncrasies of the theater and its dynamics. A play in its written form is basically a skeleton, an incomplete piece of art until it is performed on the stage. If the playwright has given detailed instructions on the set, stage directions, etc, there may not be much leeway and different versions of the same play may be fairly similar. This simplifies the problem considerably for the translator. But all too often these variables are left to the director, the stage manager, and the actors themselves, with the result that the translator may have an endless variety of versions to deal with. The deep meaning, after all, is the combination of the written play plus the acted one. In effect, the linguistic system of the play is only one of several systems that combine to produce the full meaning. Others included in the "performability" of the piece are rhythm, intonation, pitch, loudness, body language, gesture, scenery, age, appearance and athletic ability of the actors, audience reaction, etc. As with poetry, we are faced with trade-offs, but this time with an almost open-ended set of other variables.

D. TRANSLATION PROBLEMS AND TECHNIQUES.

Professional Ethics.

A translator involved in business, legal, or medical work can easily be put in a position of doing considerable good or harm through his/her efforts. Errors in this type of translation work may not be caught for a long time, if ever. The court translation profession has a number of horror stories of situations where a defendant went to jail or lost an important lawsuit because of a single mistranslated word which persuaded a judge or jury to decide in one direction or another.

The first ethical consideration of a translator is to be as competent and as well prepared as s/he possibly can, and to be honest about the limits of these abilities. A second major consideration is confidentiality. A translator frequently has access to material that could cause financial or personal damage to others, and anyone using a translator's services must be assured that confidences will be respected and honored. A translator has no right to use knowledge gained in a translation job for his/her own personal gain or enjoyment. A translator must also be aware of conflicts of interest which might arise because of personal knowledge or prior work which might be related to a translation task.

The American Translators Association (ATA) has established the following "Code of Professional Conduct and Business Practices":

As a translator, I stand between two languages and act as a bridge for the free passage of ideas from one side to the other. Because my knowledge, skill and discretion are essential to intellectual commerce, I commit myself to the highest standards of performance, ethical behavior, and sound business practice.

1. I will endeavor to translate with utmost accuracy and fidelity, so that I convey to the reader of the translation the same meaning and spirit the original conveyed to me. I acknowledge that this level of excellence requires:

a) mastery of the target language equivalent to that of an educated native speaker;

b) up-to-date knowledge of the source language and the subject area sufficient to understand the message;

c) continued efforts to improve my professional skills and to broaden and deepen my knowledge.

2. I will be truthful about my qualifications and business practices and will not accept any assignment for which I am not fully qualified, without the express consent of my client.

3. I will safeguard the interests of my clients as my own and divulge no confidential information.

4. I will derive no personal profit or financial gain from confidential information I receive in my professional capacity.

5. I will clarify all aspects of my contractual relationship with my client, preferably in writing, prior to performing an assignment and will strictly adhere to the assigned terms.

6. I will notify my client of any unresolved difficulties I may encounter in the performance of the assignment.

7. I will use a client's name as reference only if I am prepared to direct the prospective client to the individual who can attest to the quality of my work.

8. I will respect and refrain from interfering with the business relationship that exists between my client and my client's client.

9. I will refrain from unfair competitive practices.

E. COGNATES.

fc = false cognate   pc = partial cognate (be careful)
pfc = partial false cognate (be very careful)

REFUNDIDO (fc) ≠ refund; instead use "devolver."
     = consolidated or redrafted: "el borrador refundido."
REGALAR (fc) ≠ regale; instead use "agasajar."
     = to give a present.
REGULAR (pfc) = periodic and normal.
     Also = average, ordinary, moderate.
RELACION (pfc) = relationship.
     ≠ relatives; instead use "parientes."
RELEVANTE (fc) = outstanding.
     ≠ pertinent or appropriate;
     instead use "pertinente" or "relacionado."
REMARCAR (fc) = to mark again.
     ≠ to remark as in make a statement;
     instead use "decir," "notar," "observar."
REMOVER (fc) = stir.
     ≠ take away; instead use "retirar" or "quitar."
RESISTIR (pfc) = resist as in temptation.
     Also = to stand something, endure, bear: "resisto bien el frío."
RESORTE (fc) ≠ vacation resort;
     instead use "lugar de vacaciones o veraneo."
     = metallic spring of a vehicle or coil.

F. PROVERBS AND IDIOMS.

Poner la iglesia en manos de Lutero.
     To let the fox guard the chickens.
Poner la mesa   To set the table.
Ponerse colorado   To blush.
Ponerse de acuerdo   To come to an agreement.
Por adelantado   In advance; beforehand.
Por casualidad   By chance.
Por las buenas o por las malas   By hook or by crook.
Prometer el oro y el moro   To promise the moon.
Quedar bien con   To make a hit with.
Quien adelanta no mire atrás.   He who hesitates is lost.

Figure 21-3. Subjective interpretation.

LESSON 22

A. HISTORY OF TRANSLATION.

Machine Translation.

The possibility of using machines (computers) to translate is a controversial topic which has involved many claims and disappointments in the past quarter century. Its proponents have argued that the path will not be easy, but that once ambiguities are resolved and sufficiently powerful computers are developed, it will be possible to do a great deal of technical and subject-specific translation by such machines. The other side argues that for the mid and long term any such prospects are illusionary, and that even at its best machine translation is expensive, inaccurate, and requires so much post-editing (i.e., correction and polishing) by human translators that it is not worth the effort.

Proposals for machine translation surfaced before the Second World War, but serious attempts to create such machines had to wait until the development of adequate computer technology after the War. IBM and a research team at Georgetown University set up a feasibility demonstration in 1954 which led to substantial U.S. Government investment in machine translation. But the early promise did not pan out, and the products of even the most generously funded projects were generally crude and even unreadable. In 1966 the National Science Foundation set up a committee (the Automatic Language Processing Advisory Committee - ALPAC) to assess achievements and prospects. ALPAC's conclusion was that machine translation had no immediate or even future predictable prospects; it was described as slower, less accurate, and twice as expensive as human translation. Furthermore, ALPAC concluded that there was not much of a market in the U.S. for a large volume of translation, that there were adequate numbers of human translators available, and that machine translation did not justify further substantial investment of research monies and efforts. [130]

The ALPAC report was attacked by proponents of machine translation as being biased, inaccurate and distorted. But the impact of the report was dramatic and severe; funding for machine translation in the United States was sharply reduced, and progress was slowed for a number of years. However, the advent of much cheaper and more powerful computers has raised new hopes for machine translation. Advances in linguistic theory, interactive human-computer systems, word-processing, and computer aids for translation have strengthened the case for machine translation, especially in specific fields with limited ranges of subject matter.

The latter point highlights the fundamental problem of machine translation; any computer capable of handling all possible fields of human activity and imagination would have to be inconceivably complex, expensive and unwieldy. Language is humanity's most sophisticated and comprehensive cultural achievement, and to work between two or more languages in all their dimensions is a daunting task for any computer programmer. One fundamental problem is ambiguity and contextual meaning. Unless the computer is programmed to recognize and resolve all of these possibilities, then error is not only likely, but inevitable. In fact, the opponents of machine translation have frequently resorted to sometimes humorous excerpts of machine translations (some of them apocryphal) to belittle the whole process:
"The spirit is willing but the flesh is weak" =
    "The vodka is good but the meat is rotten"
"miss distance" = "señorita distancia"
"Leonardo da Vinci" = "Leonardo yes Vinci" (Russian "da" = "yes").

In the United States the major efforts at machine translation have focused on the theoretical possibilities of major breakthroughs, as well as limited applications in restricted subject fields. In such restricted fields it is possible to partially resolve the ambiguity issue by using very specific vocabulary and subject matter. U.S. Government interest has focused on translating scientific and technical material from Russian, and an important effort is also being made in the Pan American Health Organization in medical translations (English and Spanish). In these fields it is possible to drastically limit the definition of terms so as to minimize ambiguity problems.

The final product of the computer, however, frequently remains awkward and stilted, and requires considerable manipulating by translators and editors to be acceptable.

Interest in machine translation is strong in Canada, the European Community, and the Soviet Union. Canada, as a bilingual nation, has a large market for translations, and one of the more successful projects has been the machine translation of meteorological reports, with simple syntax, standardized formats, and a small vocabulary of only a couple of thousand words. Attempts in Canada to machine translate in wider fields, such as aircraft maintenance, failed and were cancelled.[131] In the European Community the challenge is even greater because of the number of languages and scope of materials involved.

One promising field is that of "computer-aided translation," in which the computer serves as a word processor with a number of features specifically designed to help the human translator. These include dictionaries, glossaries, multilanguage data banks, and thesauruses which are closely tied to the word processing program in order to permit easy access by the human translator. But the promise of machine translation is still there, awaiting further developments in computers and theoretical linguistics which some day might take much of the drudgery out of basic technical, scientific, commercial and legal translation, and perhaps free the human translator to concentrate on areas of literary and esthetic translation where the human capacity for imagination and creativity cannot be approximated by machines.

B. TRANSLATION TIDBIT.
Resort advertising[132]. Sign on the door of a Mexican tourist hotel room: "Please hang your order before retiring on your doorknob."

From a guide book to the Gascon resort of Anglet: "Whatever your tastes, and you may be fond of being alone or squashed within the madding crowd, you will find in Anglet what you may be looking for. And after you have discovered it, you will surely keep repeating for a long time."

C. THEORY OF TRANSLATION.

Theory of Machine Translation.

The basic theory of machine translation (MT) is very similar to the Larson-Nida diagram set out in Lesson 2. There are three phases: analysis of the SL, transfer between the two languages, and then synthesis of the target language. These correspond to the translation process steps of stripping SL surface structure away to get at deep meaning, transferring that deep meaning to the target language, then restructuring to get to the surface structures of the TL. From the computer's perspective, there are two basic elements: the dynamic translation program proper, which does the analysis, transfer and synthesis; and the passive component consisting of massive dictionaries to be used for finding word-for-word equivalences. The analysis of syntax is accomplished by parsing, that is, by determining the function of a given phrase and then each word in the phrase. The programs generally parse by standard types of phrases: noun phrases (NP), verb phrases (VP), prepositional phrases (PP), etc. Each of the phrases would then be broken down by its specific component and the transfer process to the TL could then begin. The diagram which follows (Figure 22-1) shows a simplified version of this parsing process as a machine translation program would attempt it.

Historically, two basic strategies were used in machine translation.[133] The first, or "direct" approach was used in most experimental MT systems up to the mid and late 1960's. It worked with a single pair of languages in one direction, taking the SL and examining all the likely words and combinations that SL would offer within the framework of the particular kinds of materials to be translated (for example, weather forecasts from French to English for the Canadian case). The basic vocabulary was defined on a one-for-one basis, with ambiguities eliminated. The syntax of the TL was simplified as much as possible to avoid ambiguities and permit a direct transfer into the corresponding TL syntax. The input syntax of the SL was formatted so as to suit the standardized needs of the TL. As can be appreciated, this approach worked reasonably well for

"The man wrote a complete program for the computer"

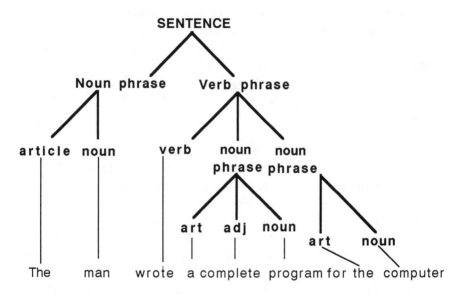

Figure 22-1: Parsing a Sentence for Machine Translation

standardized material, but would have great difficulty with anything that went outside of these parameters. The second approach, the "indirect" one, involved an intermediary language, something like a "deep meaning" language into which any one of a number of source languages or context variations could be transferred. This "deep syntactic" language would then be used to generate the appropriate surface structures in the TL.

The dictionaries which are used in MT require considerable computer memory, and are of three types: monolingual in the SL to permit analysis of the text, bilingual (SL-TL) to permit transfer, and monolingual in the TL to permit the synthesis. The dictionaries could be in an uninflected form (i.e., only the infinitive form of the verb, or the basic form of the adjective or noun), or in the complete form with all possible inflections (these dictionaries would be much larger, but would permit fast "look-up" of each word). Idiomatic expressions present special problems, and basically have to be handled on an individual basis as exceptions when they do not fit the simple forms of initial analysis. Homographs also pose special problems. These are words which have the same appearance and form, yet have different functions, such as "can the vegetable," "can do it," "in the can." To some extent the MT can identify the special uses of such words by parsing, but many exceptions have to be accounted for, with further complications in the program.

In recent years there have been advances in computers which have made MT much more attractive. For one, the long and tedious problem of input (typing the material into the computer) has been greatly simplified since many texts arrive at the MT on disks or tapes prepared by word processors and thus are ready for input to the MT without further human typing. In the case of many materials still on paper hard copy, the technology of optical character recognition (OCR) can also give the MT its data input without retyping by a human being. Editing of the output is also greatly simplified by electronic word processing, which permits direct on-screen editing instead of the old painful process of typing, making hand-written corrections, and then retyping by a human secretary.

Most advocates of MT have toned down the once exaggerated claims of the 1950's and 1960's, so that what is expected now is human-assisted machine translation. The human element comes in primarily at the post-editing stage, when a translator familiar with the material examines the MT output for errors, ambiguities, or portions that sound unnatural. Most of this post-editing is done on the word processor, with certain combinations of key strokes available for the most common functions, such as reversal of word order in noun-adjective combinations. The degree of post-editing also depends on the use of the text, especially whether it is intended for internal use for information only, or whether it is to be submitted for external publication.

D. TRANSLATION PROBLEMS AND TECHNIQUES.

Career Possibilities (including Federal) and Rates.

The student interested in career possibilities as a translator should understand that the vast majority of students who take translation courses in college do not become professional translators. The main purpose of such courses is to improve language skills and provide the student with some of the basics of translation to be used as a secondary skill. These skills should be considered as a complement to other career skills or as part of a general liberal arts education. Although it is impossible to get accurate statistics, it is probably true that most translation in the U.S. is done by non-professional translators who are asked to take on translation duties as an additional duty in their normal jobs. The quality of this translation output varies tremendously; some is good, some is terrible, and most of it is somewhere in between. Typically, a firm doing some business abroad receives correspondence in the foreign language, which is passed on to an employee who has some knowledge of that language. If none is available, then the project may be given to an outsider who is known by the firm. For the non-professional translator with language skills and the desire to use them, there are many possibilities for jobs which will call for translations skills from time to time. Any branch of the government which deals with other countries, business firms with dealings or branches abroad, research positions doing analysis on international trends, and a variety of other positions can offer this possibility. The student who is a candidate for a job with such a firm or office can enhance his/her job prospects by taking translation and language courses and getting as much practice as possible in translation.

The American Translators Association describes the principal markets for translators as follows:[134]
1. The U.S. Government and its myriad agencies;
2. U.S. and foreign "multinational" corporations and their subsidiaries;
3. U.S. importers and exporters;
4. Commercial and nonprofit research institutions;
5. Pharmaceutical, chemical, machinery, etc. manufacturers not

covered by any of the above categories;
6. Engineering and construction firms with foreign connections;
7. Patent attorneys;
8. The publishing industry;
9. The news media;
10. Municipal governments in "bilingual" U.S. cities;
11. Graduate schools of U.S. universities;
12. The United Nations and its affiliated agencies;
13. Foreign diplomatic, commercial, scientific and other
    representatives in the United States.

In the Washington, DC area there are also:
- The Organization of American States and its affiliated agencies,
such as the Inter-American Defense Board (IADB), Pan American
Health Organization (PAHO); Inter-American Development Bank
(IDB), etc.
- Lobbying groups dealing with Latin America and Hispanics in the
United States.
- Foreign embassies and agencies represented in Washington.
- Potentially, any of the over 400 offices, agencies, and other
entities listed in the Smithsonian Institution's *Scholar's Guide to
Washington: Latin American and Caribbean Studies*.

The largest single employer of part- and full-time translators in
the U.S. (and obviously in Washington) is the Federal government.
Ted Crump of the ATA[135] who is himself a government translator,
has researched Federal translation jobs and periodically reports on
his findings. He notes that it is not easy to identify all translation
positions, since a great deal of translation is being done by
individuals whose formal job title is not "translator" or "language
specialist." (This further confirms the suspicion that much
translation is done by people who primarily do something else). The
Federal agencies which do report translation positions include:
Foreign Broadcast Information Service (FBIS) and Joint Publication
Research Service (JPRS), both of which handle unclassified media
translations for the CIA; Department of State; Library of Congress
(Congressional Research Service); National Security Agency; several
agencies of the Army, Navy and Air Force; Patent and Trademark
Office (Department of Commerce); FBI; Voice of America; Social

Security Administration; and the National Institutes of Health. The pay scales for translators in the Federal Government range from GS-5 (equivalent to a clerical assistant with a high school degree) through a single position at the GS-16 level (a top grade in the Civil Service). Most translating positions are at the GS-11 to 13 grades, which corresponds to a "mid professional" level.

The single largest group of translating positions in the Federal government is in the intelligence community, especially the National Security Agency, which has a reported 1,000 translators. FBIS and JPRS do a lot of unclassified work with part-time free-lance translators, but their pay is generally considered to be below average. These two agencies have over 1,000 translators on part-time contract. Finding a Federal translation job is like getting any employment; the best leads are developed through personal and professional contacts with people inside the organization. For a student this can pose some problems, but they can be overcome through networking, translation internships, and student membership in professional organizations. The State Department frequently hires part-time escort interpreters to accompany foreign visitors on trips to the United States. For a person willing to travel, this can provide a good way to break into the T/I field. Basic qualifications include a college education, some knowledge of other countries (especially Third World), an ability to explain the United States to foreign visitors, and study or experience in fields such as international relations, cross-cultural communication, politics, government, journalism, or social work.

Literary translation is probably the most intellectually satisfying field, but the pay is generally low and the possibilities limited for all but the most gifted. Much literary translation is done on a free-lance basis by language specialists such as writers and foreign language teachers. The P.E.N. literary organization has attempted to raise the standard and rewards for literary translation, most notably in their 1970 "Manifesto on Translation,"[136] which incorporates a statement of the rights of translators. These rights include: the receiving of royalties; working under a written contract; and having the translator's name appear along with the author's.

There is much variation in pay for translation. The standard unit of measure is dollars per thousand words of text, with different pay for categories of languages and type of material (general, technical, etc). If the translator works through a translation agency, the agency may keep 40-50% of the fee charged to the client. One benchmark for establishing rates for translation is the annual "Schedule of Rates" issued by the U.S. State Department. An extract from the January 1991 schedule follows.

I. CONFERENCE SERVICES:
A. Conference interpreter (simultaneous) $325 per day
B. Translator (daily basis) $190 per day
C. Foreign language typist $105 per day

II. OTHER INTERPRETING SERVICES:
A. Foreign language escort interpreter $110-135 per day
B. English language escort interpreter $85-135 per day
C. Court interpreter $240 per day

III. TRANSLATING SERVICES:
A. Translating general material $84 per 1,000 words
B. Translating semitechnical material $90 per 1,000 words
C. Translating technical material $97 per 1,000 words
D. Typing (Roman alphabet) $15 per 1,000 words
E. Typing (non-Roman alphabet) $22 per 1,000 words
F. Review only $48-60 per 1,000 words

(Rates for translation into foreign languages are up to 50% extra).
(1,000 words is about four double-spaced typed pages).

E. COGNATES.
fc = false cognate   pc = partial cognate (be careful)
pfc = partial false cognate (be very careful)

REUNION (fc) ≠ coming together after a long time;
         instead use "reencuentro."
         = meeting.

RICO (pfc) = in terms of wealth.
But frequently has other idiomatic meanings:
"comida rica" = "delicious meal."
SALARIO (pfc) = wages, but generally only for servants, laborers.
For others, especially white collar, use "sueldo."
SALVAJE (fc) = savage.
≠ to recover a wrecked ship; instead use "salvamento."
SANCIONAR (pfc) = to apply a penalty or condemn,
almost always in a negative sense.
Generally ≠ to approve as in "the president sanctioned that
policy"; instead use "aprobar."
SANIDAD (fc) ≠ sanity; instead use "salud mental."
= sanitation.
SANO (fc) = healthy.
≠ sane; instead use "cuerdo."
SEGURIDAD (pfc) = security in sense of safety.
≠ securities in sense of stock market;
instead use "valores," or "acciones."

F. PROVERBS AND IDIOMS.

Quien fue a Sevilla perdió su silla.
Finders keepers, loosers weepers.
You went away, you lost your place.
Move your feet, lose your seat.
Quien siembra vientos recoge tempestades.
He who sows the wind reaps the whirlwind.
Reir de dientes afuera
Half-hearted laugh.
Laughing on the outside, crying on the inside.
Rendir cuentas a   To render an accounting to.
Resistirse a   To be unwilling to.
Saber a   Taste of.
Saber al dedillo   To know in great detail; have it down cold.

Figure 22-2. The perils of using translating machines.

LESSON 23

A. HISTORY OF TRANSLATION.

Professionalizing the Translation/Interpretation Field.

Translators (and more recently interpreters) have long complained that they have been taken for granted as minor collaborators of the authors they translate. Part of the problem is the slow recognition of the profession of translation/interpretation, which in turn is often the fault of translators themselves who all too frequently have been content to work for low pay and under conditions which do not enhance the profession. But developments in the field of international relations, communications, computers, and publishing suggest that we are now entering "an age of translation," in which more material is being translated and interpreted than ever before. UNESCO's *Index Translationum*, an annual bibliography which records significant translations worldwide, increased from approximately 9,000 entries in 1948 to 41,000 in 1970.[137]

The attempts to improve the professional status of translators and interpreters have been carried out by several post-War organizations which group individuals with a common interest in the field. In 1953 two European-based organizations were founded as world coordinating bodies: FIT (International Federation of Translators) and AIIC (International Association of Conference Interpreters). Two years later FIT, under the auspices of UNESCO, began to publish *Babel*, the first international journal of translation. In the United States the American Association of Language Specialists (TAALS) was founded in 1957, and in 1959 the Translation Committee of the American Center of the International PEN, and the American Translators Association (ATA) were established. This latter organization has had considerable impact on the profession through its publications, annual meetings, and accreditation program. The accreditation issue was controversial,[138] but the ATA exam has become the only generally recognized yardstick with which to establish translation credentials.

Representatives of the prestigious PEN organization from a number of nations held a Conference on Literary Translation in New York in 1970, which produced a series of important papers. These included the "Manifesto of Translation," which lamented the generally low professional status of translators, describing them as "lost children in the enchanted forest of literature."[139] The Manifesto notes that civilization would be very limited without the mutually enriching contributions made by translations, and that the capacity to receive knowledge and ideas from the past, and transmit them to future generations, depends in large measure on translation. Links to the academic world were stressed, including the recommendation that university chairs be established to teach translation on the same level as other disciplines.

Translation is in fact being taught in a growing number of universities and colleges, but there are controversies here as well. Some professional translators argue that such programs ought to be only at the graduate level, and for a small number of students who would work in the field only when highly qualified. Language teachers in the academic world tend to take a different view, believing that translation should be taught as a secondary skill for students majoring in languages or related fields such as international relations or international business, inasmuch as professionals in these fields are frequently called upon to perform translations as part of their jobs. There appears to be room for both of these approaches, and recent publications of the ATA have reflected a convergence of views in this regard.

B. TRANSLATION TIDBIT.

Many names of Western U.S. states have Spanish origins. Some are obvious, some not. California may be a corruption of two Latin words, "calida fornax," meaning, "hot furnace or oven." Arizona is apparently a corruption of "árida zona." Oregon could come from a description of the Indians as "orejones."

Many names for females in Spanish end in "o" and would thus seem to be masculine: Consuelo, Amparo, Socorro. The explanation is that the full name includes the name of the Virgin Mary, as in "María del Consuelo," "María del Amparo," "María del Socorro."[140]

C. THEORY OF TRANSLATION.

The "Prime Reader."

A major consideration for the translator is who will be the "prime reader," or principal audience for his/her work, since the nature of this "prime reader" will affect many translation procedures and approaches. If the translator is working for a single client, the prime reader will probably be known to the translator, and will specify the purpose of the task in ways that will be helpful to the translator. For example, the client may indicate that a final and fully polished work is desired so as to permit publication (or even camera-ready printing) without additional editing. Or the client may only want a summary of the TL text, sometimes known as a "quick" translation. The translator should be cautious with this latter category, however, since if s/he is careless, his/her reputation may suffer. It is also good to know whether the target audience is a single individual or many, and if the latter, whether the readership is likely to be heterogeneous or homogeneous in terms of the characteristics which are detailed below.

Larson[141] has laid out a very useful set of criteria to define the target audience and to assist the translator in adjusting to that audience. She argues that the principal characteristics of the audience which affect how the translator approaches the task are: level of education, age, occupation, knowledge of the subject, cultural differences, circumstances of use, degree of bilingualism, and language attitudes. To this might be added the degree to which the target audience is already familiar with the material, or has had access to it in the original.

Once armed with a profile of the audience in terms of the above characteristics, Larson argues that there are four variables which the translator can use to fit the target audience. These are: choice of vocabulary; choice of grammatical constructions; implicit information to be made explicit (and explicit information which could be dropped); and use of supplementary material, such as footnotes, glossaries, parenthetical commentary, etc. Equipped with this information and the choices before him/her, the translator can then set the register of the material, make the choices which would best insure a fit between the translation and the target audience, and proceed with the task. After completion, it would be wise to try the product out on one or more representative individuals from the target audience to see if the fit is a good one. If the need to insure a good fit for the prime reader is important, a questionnaire can be set up for a test prime reader to see how much of the subject matter is understood. Additional questions might try to find out the impression made in the test prime reader's mind as to who the writer was, and what his/her level of education, age, and occupation were. If the feedback matches the assumptions made by the translator, there is a considerably higher chance that the translation will be a successful one.

Despite all the advice to make his/her translation fit the prime reader's needs, the translator also needs to remember that, like the author, s/he will be judged in future years by the written word that remains behind ("scripta manet -- verba volant"). It is equally important to resist undertaking translation jobs that are beneath one's professional status, or which might be embarrassing in years to come.

D. TRANSLATION PROBLEMS AND TECHNIQUES.

The ATA and "Profile of a Translator."

The American Translators Association is the largest, best organized and most helpful of the professional organizations. From their headquarters in Ossining, NY they organize an annual meeting, produce a monthly newsletter (The ATA Chronicle), and administer the accreditation exam and certificate. The ATA has a number of local chapters, including a very active one in the Washington, DC area, which publishes its own newsletter (Capital Translator), and administers the ATA accreditation exam along with a workshop to prepare candidates for the exam. Both the ATA and the chapter have "associate member" status for students, with lowered annual fees.

The following has been extracted from materials contained in the ATA's publication, "Profile of a Competent Translator and of an Effective Translator Training Program":

A. WHAT STANDARDS SHOULD TRANSLATORS MEET?

1. A highly developed sense of intellectual integrity, responsibility, and ethical conduct, which in practical terms means:

a. Not accepting assignments beyond one's language and/or subject matter competence;

b. Continuing the ongoing process of self-education and improvement (in terms of current developments both in linguistic usage and scientific/technical advances);

c. Bringing unresolved problems to the client's attention (eschewing guesswork);

d. Keeping unpublished information the translator is commissioned to translate confidential;

e. Respecting deadlines mutually agreed to;

f. Helping upgrade the performance of the profession as a whole;

g. Sharing knowledge with one's colleagues;

h. Refraining from unseemly or exaggerated promotional claims;

i. Abstaining from unsolicited criticism of translations by others.

2. Language and subject-matter requirements:

a. Sound knowledge of source language, equivalent to at least 4 years of intensive and 10 years of sporadic study;

b. Above-average writing ability in the target language, equivalent to that of (self or otherwise) educated native speakers;

c. Reasonable familiarity with the subject matter, equivalent to that which can be acquired by at least one year (preferably two) of formal education or job experience in the particular field;

d. Access to recent reference books, equivalent to those found in a fairly up-to-date professional library, and assiduous consultation thereof;

e. Contact with more experienced fellow translators or more knowledgeable linguists and scientists, and the willingness to consult with them (on a reciprocal basis).

B. WHAT TRAINING IS REQUIRED TO ATTAIN STANDARDS?

1. The following curriculum would seem to be the best way for a college student to prepare for a career in translating:

a. Courses that provide an extensive knowledge of, and ability to reason in, the subject matter of the translation: mathematics, pure sciences, social sciences, history, business administration and economics;

b. Courses that provide a sound reading knowledge and grasp of the language(s) from which one will be translating: 4 years of a major language, 2 years of a minor language; and as many basic language courses as possible; at least 2 years of Latin (if nothing else, it will do wonders for one's English);

c. Courses that provide the ability to express oneself in lucid and straightforward English: writing courses, including one in newspaper writing and one in technical writing.

2. Periodic participation in advanced "postgraduate" workshops, notably in specialized subject matter area.

C. WHAT TRANSLATION FIELDS HAVE SPECIAL REQUISITES?

1. **Literary** requires:

a. Above-average knowledge of the source language;

b. Highly developed writing ability in the target language;

c. Comprehensive background in the culture (specifically, the literature), history and social customs of other countries (notably that of the source language).

Rewards: intellectual satisfaction, public exposure, reasonable deadlines, byline credit.

Drawbacks: limited economic opportunities ("feast or famine") because of limited market and generally lower rates than in other fields of translation; lack of retirement benefits (unless working in a salaried position).

2. **Scientific/Technical** requires:

a. Moderately extensive scientific/technical knowledge;

b. Familiarity with specific terminology (and, in the absence thereof, to "know when you don't know");

c. A reasonably up-to-date sci-tech library;

d. Access to reproduction facilities (for graphs and figures);

e. In most cases, impeccable typing ability and good layout sense (or an associate typist who has these attributes).

Rewards: fairly steady income, with generally higher rates than in the field of literary translation and a broad market, with the opportunity to expand one's subject matter knowledge.

Drawbacks: often "impossible" deadlines, the necessity of being a "Jack/Jane of all subjects," fairly high cost of reference books, lack of retirement benefits (unless working in a salaried position).

3. Commercial requires: most of the same qualifications as scientific/technical translation, but perhaps to a lesser degree (except for the bane of deadlines, which must often be met "by yesterday").

In addition to the above "profile" indicated by the ATA, we could add that a competent professional translator:

- Has access, and preferably owns, a personal computer with a good word processing program and a high-quality printer. The word-processing program should include a Spanish font and dictionary, as well as spell-checking and word-counting features.
- Is an active participant and member of the ATA and local chapter.
- Does what s/he can to bridge the gap between the academic and working fields of translation by teaching, organizing workshops, or lecturing in language and translation classes.
- Does some "pro bono" work for free, or at low fees, for deserving organizations.
- Is accredited by the ATA (i.e., has passed the ATA accreditation exam).
- Is registered in the ATA or local chapter's "Professional Services Directory."
- Maintains a file of completed and published work as well as letters from satisfied clients.

E. COGNATES.

fc = false cognate   pc = partial cognate (be careful)
pfc = partial false cognate (be very careful)

SENSIBLE (fc) ≠ sensible; instead use "sensanto," "razonable."
    = sensitive.

SENTENCIA (pfc) = jail sentence.
≠ grammatical sentence; instead use "frase" or "oración. "
SERIO (pfc) = serious (in the sense of grave).
But also = reliable, professional, worthwhile.
SIMPATICO (fc) ≠ sympathetic; instead use "compasivo" or
"dispuesto a. "
= pleasant, nice, attractive personality.
SOLICITUD (pfc) = solicitude.
Also = application form.
SUBURBIO (pfc) = suburb, but there is a cultural and economic
difference in that "suburbs" in many Latin American cities are
the low-class shanty-towns while the central city is the
wealthier and more elegant section. The reverse is true in many
U.S. cities. Thus, in certain circumstances, "suburbio" =
slum.

F. PROVERBS AND IDIOMS.
Sacar en limpio   To come up with a final version; to know fully.
Salirse con la suya   To have one's way; to get away with it.
Salon de actos   Auditorium.
Saltar a la vista   To be obvious.
Según el caso   According to the situation; it all depends.
Según mi entender   As I understand it.
Sentir en el alma   To feel deeply.
Ser aficionado a   To be fond of; a fan of.
Serle a uno indiferente   To be immaterial to one.
Sin fin de   Numberless; infinite.
Sin novedad   Nothing new.
Sin ton ni son   Hopeless.
Sudar la gota gorda   To have a hard time; sweat it out.
Tener antipatía   To dislike.
Tener fama de   To have the reputation of.
Tener la palabra   To have the floor to speak.

LESSON 24

A. HISTORY OF TRANSLATION.

Gregory Rabassa, Contemporary Translator.

The best-known contemporary Spanish-English translator is Gregory Rabassa, who has done much to popularize Latin American literature in the United States as well as to increase the prestige of the translation profession generally. While Rabassa is best-known for his translations of the Colombian novelist Gabriel García Márquez, he has also rendered into English the works of a number of other prominent Latin American writers, including Miguel Angel Asturias of Guatemala, Julio Cortázar and Luisa Valenzuela of Argentina, Mario Vargas Llosa of Peru, Jorge Amado and Clarice Lispector of Brazil, Dmitri Aguilera-Malta of Ecuador, Luis Rafael Sánchez of Puerto Rico and José Lezama Lima of Cuba.

His work with García Márquez includes everything in English by that author, except for the author's first book. The best known of his translations is *One Hundred Years of Solitude*, (1970) which is generally credited with doing more than any other current book to arouse the interest of English speakers in Latin American literature. The novel would appear to be a difficult one to translate because of its magic realism and the ethereal visions of the Buendía family in the small and imaginary Colombian Caribbean town of Macondo. But Rabassa disagrees, saying that it was in fact relatively easy to translate because of a style which "almost translates itself."[142] García Márquez' reaction to the translation is well-known; he has said that he prefers Rabassa's English translation to his own Spanish original. Rabassa replied that the remark was "probably less of a compliment to my translation than it is to the English language."[143]

His first major translation project was Julio Cortázar's *Hopscotch*, a difficult book to translate because of the many puns and word-plays. In one of them Cortázar refers to the "Irreal

Academia Española," which Rabassa translated as the "Roil Spanish Academy." Rabassa cited this as an example of the technique of giving up the literal word for word translation and instead attempting to find a word play with approximately the same equivalent impact. In a recent translation workshop in Washington[144] Rabassa argued somewhat facetiously that he, and all other translators, were basically frauds because "everything is untranslatable." Rabassa stressed the links between language and culture, giving as one example the expression frequently used by Mexican peasants, "es que...," as in "es que somos muy pobres." He cited this as a cultural gesture of humility on the part of a sector of Mexican society that has learned the need to be deferential to the powerful. At the same workshop Rabassa noted a problem he had translating the name of a cheap liquor sold on the north coast of Colombia which appears in Gabriel García Márquez' *Crónica de una Muerte Anunciada*. The brand is "Gordolobo," which is a word coined from Gordon's dry gin and the "lobo" which appears on the label (the figure is actually a boar). After much puzzling on how to translate the term, Rabassa settled on the colloquial English term, "rot gut."

Rabassa mentions that in translating Cortazar's *Hopscotch*, a typographical error on his part ("fired egg" for "fried egg") was accepted by the author as being more appropriate than his own original Spanish version. Also from the same work came the problem of how to translate Cortazar's characterization of secret policemen with a string of ingenious alliterative words, using profuse Spanish diminutives and augmentatives, which created images of the agents as ants: hormigón, hormigucho, and so forth. Rabassa's solution was a different but equally effective English word-play: domin-ant, sycoph-ant, miscre-ant.

B. TRANSLATION TIDBIT.
A company in Colombia wanted to buy a product abroad and advertised in an international journal. There were three responses. An American company replied, sending a brochure in English. A German company replied with a brochure in Spanish. A Japanese company sent a team to Bogotá to make a personal presentation in Spanish to the directors. Guess which company made the sale?[145]

C. THEORY OF TRANSLATION.

Translation: Art, Craft, or Science?

There has been some debate in recent years over whether translation is an art, a science, or a craft. In truth, it has elements of all of these: art, because it is creative, humanistic, and sensitive to cultural nuances; science because of its links to the discipline of linguistics, and the existence of certain rules, procedures and techniques; and craft because of the leeway the individual translator has to shape and polish her/his work in accordance with experience and feel for the balance between esthetics and function. The answer to the rhetorical question also depends on the type of translation involved.

The case for translation as art resides primarily in the literary field, and especially in the translation of poetry. The creative act involved in good literature, and the strong feeling that language is inherently one of the liberal arts, combine to give this type of translation the "feel" of art. The translator has been described as a sort of creative magician, achieving the seemingly impossible by preserving the creative genius of the original author and somehow performing acts of alchemy on it to make it something else without changing its essence. At the same time the translator must sacrifice and limit his/her own creativity by not putting his personal stamp on the re-forged work of literary art. This kind of translation is "like every kind of art, an act of grace."[146]

Translation as craft shifts the emphasis to the careful use of complex verbal tools and then to the molding and polishing of the semi-finished product to achieve that seemingly impossible balance between faithfulness to the original and elegance. Not all of the craftsmanship is this careful, of course. There are translation hacks who turn out inferior products at low prices because there are prime readers who will tolerate this, or who simply do not want to pay more for what they consider to be a low-level mechanical task. These prime readers deserve what they get, but unfortunately this does not do much for the profession.

The claims of translation as science rest heavily on the theoretical aspects of the discipline of linguistics, and on the possibilities that the computer holds for machine translation. The "science" of translation is still shaky, and will remain so until linguistics can make more direct and unambiguous contributions to the practical problems facing the translator. In some ways the situation is analogous to what medicine was in the Middle Ages before the Renaissance and modern sciences (chemistry, physics, anatomy) gave it a more solid base. Science demands measurement, laws and replicability; neither linguistics nor translation theory can yet provide these in clear enough fashion to make translation the science that some of the more ardent proponents of this view desire. Transformational grammar and some of the programs written for machine translation come close, but there is still a long way to go, as the need for the post-editor's craft and art make clear.

For the moment it is thus perhaps most useful to conceive of translation as containing features of all three categories: art, craft and science. Depending on whether we are translating a poem, a newspaper article or a standardized weather report, we may be more inclined to lean in one direction or the other. But most translators will work with a fairly wide range of material, and an appreciation of translation as art, craft, and science can make the task easier, more satisfying, and more enjoyable.

D. TRANSLATION PROBLEMS AND TECHNIQUES.

The ATA Accreditation Exam.

The accreditation exam and certificate administered by the American Translators Association is the only nationally-recognized professional credential of its type other than the Federal court interpreter's exam and certificate. The ATA exam was set up in 1972 and has expanded its combination of languages steadily since then. Spanish-English and English-Spanish are among the most popular of the language pairs. The exam is open-book, and candidates are encouraged to bring mono-lingual as well as general and specialized bi-lingual dictionaries. Five passages of approximately 500 words each are presented to the candidate in the following categories: general, literary, legal or business, scientific or medical, and semi-technical. The candidate selects three of the five passages to be completed in the three-hour time frame. Grading is done by two professional translators who know the candidate only by an anonymous number. To pass, the graders must agree that the candidate has performed satisfactorily in at least two of three passages (if there is disagreement a third grader is called in). A given passage is "failed" if it contains two major errors or one major error and six or seven minor ones. Major errors consist of omission or significant mistakes in substantive material. This can be a title, a paragraph number, quantities, or an important modifier.

The following suggestions were prepared by the author of this text for a workshop conducted by the Washington, DC, chapter of the American Translators Association.

1. Preparation for the exam:
a. Read as wide a range of materials in both languages as you can.
b. Develop a list of equivalent (not literal) colloquial expressions, sayings, similes, and metaphors.
c. Keep and review your past translation work, especially if it has been edited or corrected by someone else whose work you respect.
d. Prepare a list of false cognates, become familiar with them, and the contexts in which they will give you trouble.

2. Bring to the Examination:
a. A good general Spanish-English dictionary
b. Specialized Spanish-English dictionaries in the following areas: medical, technical, scientific, business, politics.
c. Good single-language (i.e., English-only and Spanish-only) dictionaries which will give you definitions of words.
d. An ample supply of black ball-point pens. Remember that you need to make good copies for at least two readers.

3. Making your choice of 3 out of 5 passages.
(A few minutes spent on a wise decision here may save you grief later on during the exam).
a. Read all five passages quickly to get a sense of their difficulty.

b. Other things being equal, you are probably better off choosing technical, scientific and medical subjects over literary ones. Even though the vocabulary in technical-scientific-medical passages may be more difficult, the syntax and grammar are probably straight-forward and you should be able to solve the vocabulary problems using your dictionaries. Literary passages may contain heavy doses of metaphor, symbolism, idioms, and other devices which tend to obscure the meaning. Even the punctuation in literary passages may be more complicated and tricky.

4. Steps in doing the translation.
a. Read your selected passage quickly and completely, looking for general meaning.
b. Read it a second time, looking for words you are unsure about. Look the words up in your dictionaries. If a word is not in your dictionary, but you are pretty sure of its grammatical function (usually a noun), and you understand the general sense of the passage, you might want to use the device of stating that it is "not in my dictionary."
c. To be sure that you have caught the "deep meaning," sit back and make a mental precis (summary) of the passage.
d. Begin translating by sentences or short paragraphs. Translate each "block" of text in your mind first, then in writing. Don't waste time doing a rough draft since you are allowed to make neat corrections and changes in your final text.
e. Check for spelling, punctuation, titles, headings.
f. Set it aside, do the second and third passage, then come back and re-read it for style and errors.
g. One strategy is to do your easiest passage first, and do it quickly. Don't agonize over shades of meaning. Save your time for the hardest passage, where your agonizing may be more productive.

5. Some common errors to watch out for:
a. Leaving out a title, a specific quantity, or a significant modifier. These are usually due to carelessness, but they are "major."
b. Don't be either too literal or too "free" in your translation. Do not try to add, clarify, explain, or omit material. Don't use alternate translations.
c. Be on guard for false cognates.

d. Be aware of the different use of verb tenses in English and Spanish (i.e, Spanish use of the "historical present"; Spanish imperfect and preterite uses; Spanish future can be a command, etc).
e. Be careful not to over-use the article in English.
f. Be familiar with the relationship between the Spanish reflexive and the English passive voice.
g. Watch the decimal point=comma equivalence, and the problems with numbers, such as "mil millones = a billion."

6. Are you ready for the exam?
The exam involves a fair commitment of your time, money, effort, and pride. There is little point in attempting it if you realistically don't have a decent chance to pass it. If you are trying to translate into a language that is not your first language, you are a high-risk candidate unless you have a lot of experience. Try a sample test first and see how you do. See if you can convince a typical native speaker that what you have translated was written by a native speaker.

7. Finally, relax.
The examiners are not looking for perfection. You are permitted one major error or five or six minor ones in each passage, and you have to pass two of the three passages. There are allowances for some subjectivity, and there is no "single solution."

E. COGNATES.
fc = false cognate   pc = partial cognate (be careful)
pfc = partial false cognate (be very careful)

SUCESO (fc) ≠ success; instead use "éxito."
        = event.
SUTIL (pfc) = implies more craftiness than in the English.
SUJETO (pfc) = generally same as English, but when referring to a
        person, can have negative implications:
        "este sujeto es sospechoso."
TERMINOS (pfc) = terms as in words: "es un término técnico."
        ≠ conditions; instead use "condiciones":
        " condiciones del tratado."

TIPO (pfc) = type as in pattern, classification or model.
  Also = colloquial "guy," "fellow": "es un tipo muy simpático."
TUTOR (pfc) = private teacher.
  Also = guardian.
ULTIMO (fc) = final or last.
  ≠ definitive; instead use "definitivo."
URBANO (pfc) = urban (city)
  ≠ urbane; instead use "cortés," "sofisticado."
UTILIDADES (pfc) = profits of a business.
  ≠ house utilities (gas, electricity, water);
  use "servicios públicos."
VAGO (pfc) = vague as in imprecise.
  Also = lazy; also is colloquial for "vagabond."
VOTO (pfc) = to vote as a political act.
  Also = promise or vow.

F. PROVERBS AND IDIOMS.

Tener presente   To keep in mind.
Tocante a   Regarding.
Tocar en lo vivo   To cut to the quick.
Tocarle a uno   To be one's turn.
Tomar cuerpo   To take shape.
Tomarse el trabajo de   To take the trouble to.
Trabar amistad   To strike up a friendship.
Trato hecho   It's a deal.
Tropezar con   To stumble across; to run into.
Un no sé qué   A certain air; a certain something.
Una golondrina no hace el verano.
  A swallow does not a summer make.
Valer la pena   To be worthwhile.
Velar por   To watch out for; to care for.
Ver es creer.   Seeing is believing.
Y pico   And a little bit.
Zapatero a tus zapatos.
  Mind your own business. Shoemaker, stick to your last.

NOTES

1. *The Encyclopedia Americana*, vol. 3, 1960 edition, p. 5.

2. Edouard Roditi, *Interpreting: Its History in a Nutshell* (Washington: Georgetown University Center for Translation and Interpretation, 1982) p. 1.   Ruth A. Roland, *Translating World Affairs* (Jefferson, N.C.: McFarland & Co., 1982) p. 27.

3. Roland, *Translating World Affairs*, pp. 28-29.

4. Roland, *Translating World Affairs*, p. 29.

5. George Steiner, *After Babel: Aspects of Language and Translation* (N.Y. and London: Oxford University Press, 1975) p. 240.   Roditi, *Interpreting*, p. 2.

6. Octavio Paz, *Traducción: Literatura y Literalidad* (Barcelona: Tusqueta Editor, 1971) p. 7.

7. Marcy S. Powell, "Traduttore, Traditore," *Verbatim*, Summer 1983, p. 1.

8. Cited in Steiner, *After Babel*, p. 242. The translation is by T. Cribb.

9. Valentín García Yebra, *Teoría y Práctica de la Traducción* (Madrid: Gredos, 1984) p. 721.

10. García Yebra, *Teoría*, pp. 723-4.

11. Valentín García Yebra, *En Torno a la Traducción* (Madrid: Gredos, 1983) p. 61.   Eugene A. Nida, *Towards a Science of Translation* (Leiden: E.J. Brill, 1964) pp. 12-13. Robert Boughner, "Jerome's Legacy to Translators," *Jerome Quarterly*, November-December 1986, pp. 5-7.

12. Roland, *Translating World Affairs*, p. 118.

13. Mildred Larson, *Meaning-Based Translation* (Lanham: University Press of America, 1984) Chapter 1, especially pp. 3-6.

14. Eugene Nida, *Language, Structure and Translation* (Stanford: Stanford University Press, 1975) pp. 79-81.   For a critique, see Louis Kelly, *The True Interpreter: a History of Translation* (Oxford: Basil, Blackwell, 1979) Chapter 2.

15. George Steiner, *After Babel: Aspects of Language and Translation* (N.Y. and London: Oxford University Press, 1975) pp. 117-118.

16. Cicero, cited in Bassnett-McGuire, *Translation Studies*, p. 43.

17. Jacobsen, cited in Bassnett-McGuire, *Translation Studies*, p. 43.

18. Suzanne Levine, "Notes on Translation," *Review*, Winter 1971, p. 93.

19. Adapted from Larson, *Meaning-Based Translation*, p. 17.

20. Cited in Marilyn Gaddis Rose, ed. *Translation Spectrum: Essays in Theory and Practice* (Albany: SUNY, 1981) p. 32.

21. García Yebra, *En Torno*, Chapter 11.   Mariano García-Landa, "The Toledo School," *El País* (Madrid), 10 January 1981.

22. García Yebra, *En Torno*, pp. 314-315.

23. Mariano Brasa Diez, "Alfonso X el Sabio y los Traductores Españoles," *Cuadernos Hispanoamericanos*, August 1984, 410: pp. 21-33

24. *Swissair News*, 9 September 1980, p. 1.

25. Nida, *Towards a Science of Translation*, especially Chapter 6.   Nida, *Language, Structure and Translation*, pp. 250-1.   Eugene A. Nida. & W. D. Reyburn, *Meaning Across Cultures*, especially Chapter 2.

26. Nida, *Language, Structure and Translation*, pp. 250.

27. Dolet's principles can be found in Nida, *Towards a Science of Translation*, pp. 15-16.

28. Nida, *Towards a Science of Translation*, pp. 14-16.

29. *Swissair News*, 19 September 1988, p. 1.

30. Nida, *Towards a Science of Translation*, p. 145.

31. Theodore H. Savory, *The Art of Translation* (London: Jonathan Cape, 1968) p. 49.

32. Larson, *Meaning Based Translation*, pp. 95-96.

33. Nida, *Towards a Science of Translation*, pp. 14-15. Roditi, *Interpreting*, p. 6.   For Pigafetta and the penguins, see George Gaylord Simpson, *Penguins Past and Present, Here and There* (New Haven: Yale University Press, 1976).

34. Shirley Brice Heath, *Telling Tongues: Language Policy in Mexico - Colony to Nation* (N.Y.: Columbia Teacher's College Press, 1972) p. 6.   Nida, *Language, Structure and Translation*, p. 213.

35. Heath, *Telling Tongues*, pp. 1-5.

36. Personal observation, Chinchón, Spain, May 1984.

37. Larson, *Meaning Based Translation*, pp. 95-96.

38. Larson, *Meaning Based Translation*, pp. 436-7.

39. Humberto Valencia, "Point of View : Avoiding Hispanic Market Blunders," *Journal of Advertising Research*, December 1983, p. 21.

40. Fortune, "If you want a big new Market...," *Fortune*, 21 November 1988, pp. 181-188.

41. Fortune, "If you want a big new Market...," p. 181.

42. For sources of these ads, see Valencia, "Point of View," Fortune, "If you want a big new Market...," and Michel Coclet, "Translating Advertising Copy," in *ATA Proceedings*, 26th Annual Conference, Miami, 1985.

43. Heath, *Telling Tongues*, p. 11.

44. Roland, *Translating*, p. 63.

45. Roman Jakobson, "On Linguistic Aspects of Translation," in Rueben A Brower, *On Translating* (N.Y.: Oxford University Press, 1966) p. 233.

46. Henry G. Schogt, *Linguistics, Literary Analysis, and Literary Translation* (Toronto: University of Toronto Press, 1988) p. 3.

47. Ann E. Bennaton, "Please don't F*** the Grass," *Verbatim*, Spring 1984, pp. 13-14.

48. Roland, *Translating*, p. 64-65.

49. Susana Jakfalvi-Leiva, *Traducción, Escritura y Violencia Colonizadora: Un Estudio de la Obra del Inca Garcilaso* (Syracuse: Maxwell School of Citizenship and Public Affairs, 1984) p. 59.

50. Provided by the Washington Opera Society, May 1978.

51. Peter Newmark, *Approaches to Translation*. (N.Y.: Pergamon, 1982) p. 148.

52. Heath, *Telling Tongues*, pp. 5, 12, 14-16, 44, 49, 179-180.   Miguel Leon-Portilla, "Translating the Amerindian Texts," *Latin American Indian Literatures*, Fall 1983, p. 101.

53. Nida, Language, *Structure and Translation*, pp. 213-215.

54. *ATA Chronicle*, October 1983.

55. Gerardo Vázquez-Ayora, *Introducción a la Traductología* (Washington: Georgetown University Press, 1977) pp. 289-312.

56. Roger J. Steiner, *Two Centuries of Spanish and English Bilingual Lexicography (1590-1800)* (The Hague: Mouton, 1970). Mario Pei, *What's in a Word?* (N.Y.: Hawthorn Books, 1968) Chapter 8.

57. Consuelo Lopez-Morillas, *The Qur'an in 16th Century Spain* (London: Tamesis Books, 1982).

58. See also Elizabeth Welt Trahan, "The Arabic Translator in Don Quijote," in *Translation Perspectives*, ed. Marilyn Gaddis Rose (Binghampton: SUNY, 1984) pp. 71-85.

59. Lincoln Canfield, *East Meets West South of the Border* (Carbondale: Southern Illinois University Press, 1968) p. 116.

60. Vazquez-Ayora, *Traductología*, pp. 266-272.

61. Harold Simon, "Translation and Interpretation for Ethnomedical Conditions," in *ATA Proceedings* (26th Annual Conference, Miami, 1985) pp. 115-117.

62. As cited in Hubert Herring, *A History of Latin America* (N.Y.: Knopf, 1965) pp. 176-177.

63. Pedro R. León, "Pedro de Cieza de León, príncipe maltratado," *Revista de Indias*, July-December 1971, pp 210-217.

64. Canfield, *East Meets West*, p. 122.

65. Vázquez-Ayora, *Traductología*, p. 334-366.

66. Marilyn Frankenthaler, *Skills for Bilingual Legal Personnel* (Cincinnati: South-Western Publishing Co., 1982).

67. See Jack Child, *Spanish Translation: International Relations of Latin America* (Experimental text, The American University, 1985) especially Section E.

68. See Jo Ann Englebert "Translation for Legal Personnel," in Frankenthaler, *Skills for Bilingual Legal Personnel.*

69. Englebert "Translation," pp. 235-236.

70. Steiner, *English Translation Theory*, pp. 1-3.

71. Dryden cited in Nida, *Towards a Science*, pp. 17-18.

72. As cited in Savory, *The Art of Translation*, p. 43.

73. Letter from American University graduate student, L.C.W., 14 February 1989.

74. *ATA Chronicle*, July 1985, p. 5.

75. *Newsweek*, 14 December 1987, p. 9.

76. *Washington Post*, 3 September 1986, p. A4.

77. *Washington Post*, 24 October 1984, p. 1.

78. Bassnett-McGuire, *Translation Studies*, pp. 65-66.

79. Shelley as cited in Bassnett-McGuire, *Translation Studies*, pp. 65-66.

80. *Capitol Translator*, vol. V, no. 9, October 1984.

81. Gregory Rabassa, "The Silk Purse Business: A Translator's Conflicting Responsibilities," in Frawley, *Translation*, pp. 35-36.

82. Nida has used this technique extensively; see his *Towards a Science of Translation* and *The Theory and Practice of Translation*. Also, R. David Zorc, "Translatability and Non-Translatability Between Languages and Cultures: a Case for Semantic Mapping," in F. Eppert, *Papers on Translation* (SEAMO, 1983).

83. I am indebted to my friend and colleague Leonel Antonio de la Cuesta for much of this material on Martí, taken from a presentation he made at the 1985 ATA convention in Miami.

84. José Martí, *Argentina y la Primera Conferencia Panamericana* (Buenos Aires: Editorial Transición, n.d.).

85. Kessel Schwarts, "A Source for Three Martí Letters: The Art of Translation," *Revista de Estudios Hispánicos*, January 1984, pp. 133-153.

86. Leonel de la Cuesta, "Martí Traductor- Apuntes Liminares" (Conferencia), *ATA Convention Proceedings* (Miami: ATA, 1985) pp. 6-7.

87. Powell, "Traduttore, Traditore," p. 17.

88. García Yebra, *Teoría y Práctica de la Traducción*, p. 353.

89. García Yebra, *Teoría*, Chapter X.   President Ricardo J. Alfaro, *Diccionario de Anglicismos* (Madrid: Gredos, 1964). Chris Pratt, *El Anglicismo en el Español Peninsular Contemporáneo* (Madrid: Gredos, 1980).   Grace Tillinghast, "¿Qué Pasa con el Español?" in American Translators Association, *Silver Tongues* (Ossining, N.Y.: ATA) 1984

90. Bassnett-McGuire, *Translation Studies* , pp. 72-73.

91. Roland, *Translation*, pp. 77-78.

92. *ATA Chronicle*, October 1983.

93. Clinton C. Carney, *A Guide to Translating for the Spanish and English Bilingual* (Panama: Litografía Enan, 1988) pp. 73-75.

94. Pei, Mario, *What's in a Word?* (N.Y.: Hawthorn Books, 1968) p. 76.

95. Basil Thompson, *Ramón Writes* (Buenos Aires: The Buenos Aires Herald, 1979). The author of this text, who grew up in Argentina, remembers speaking in Ramon's style with Anglo-Argentine friends.

96. From Owen's preface to his translation of Estanislao del Campo's gauchesque poem "El Fausto," as cited in John Walker, "Walter Owen: The Latin American Epic and the Art of Translation," *Latin American Literary Review*, Fall 74, pp. 51-64. Walter Owen, translator, *Martín Fierro* (N.Y.: Farrar & Rinehart, 1936) p. 11.

97. From Owen's preface to *Martín Fierro*, p. 12.

98. Walter Owen, (translator) *La Araucana*, by Ercilla y Zuniga; preface to translation. (Buenos Aires, 1906) pp. XX to XXI.

99. Owen, (translator) *La Araucana*, p. XXVI.

100. Owen, (translator) *La Araucana*, p. XXVII.

101. Nida, *Language, Structure*, pp. 174-5, 215.

102. Bassnett-McGuire, *Translation Studies*, pp. 23-29.

103. Larson, *Translation*, pp. 252-4.

104. See, for example the section on "common idioms and proverbs" in the University of Chicago's *Spanish-English Dictionary*, or specialized dictionaries such as A. Daniel Hughes, *Slang 5000 Modismos del Inglés* (Mexico: Diana: 1986). Eugene Savaiano, *2001 Spanish and English Idioms* (N.Y.: Barron's Educational Series, 1976).

105. Alan Duff, *The Third Language: Recurrent Problems of Translation into English* (N.Y.: Pergamon Institute of English, 1981) pp. 95-96.

106. Heath, *Telling Tongues*, pp. 101-3, 112.

107. *Washington Post*, 22 February 1986, p. G-10.

108. *Parade Magazine*, 10 July 1988, 28 August 1988.

109. Newmark, *Approaches to Translation*, p. 121.

110. Jo Ann Englebert, in Frankenthaler, *Skills*, p. 201.

111. Bassnett-McGuire, *Translation Studies*. Vázquez-Ayora, *Traductología*.

112. Paz, *Traducción*, p. 13.

113. *Swissair News*, 19 September 1980.

114. Duff, *Third Language*.

115. Roland, *Translating*, p. 109.

116. Roland, *Translating*, p. 113.

117. David Ricks, "Pitfalls in Advertising Overseas," *Journal of Advertising Research*, December 1974, pp. 47-50.

118. Danica Seleskovitch, *Interpreting for International Conferences* (Washington: Pen and Booth, 1978) p. 9.

119. Seleskovitch, *Interpreting*, p. 9. Robert Ekvall, *Faithful Echo* (N.Y.: Twayne Publishers, 1960).

120. U.S. State Department, *State*, January 1987, pp. 13-14.

121. *Time Magazine*, 29 May 1989, p. 65.

122. John Leeth, *The Court Interpreter Examination* (Washington: Georgetown University Center for Translation and Interpretation, 1982?) pp. 2-4.

123. *Verbatim*, Autumn 1984, p. 6.

124. Bassnett-McGuire, *Translation Studies*, pp. 83-87.

125. Dudley Fitts, "The Poetic Nuance," in Rueben A Brower, *On Translating* (N.Y.: Oxford University Press, 1966) p. 33.

126. Fitts, "The Poetic Nuance," p. 35-38.

127. John Felstiner, *Translating Neruda* (Stanford: Stanford University Press, 1980).

128. James S. Holmes, ed, *The Nature of Translation* (Bratislava: International Conference on Translation as an Art, 1968) pp. 91-95.

129. García Yebra, *En Torno a la Traducción*, pp. 139-140.

130. W. J. Hutchins, "Machine Translation and Machine-aided Translation," in William Frawley, *Translation* (Newark: University of Delaware Press, 1984). Fred Klein, "Automatic Translation of Natural Languages," *Capital Translator*, May 1985, p. 5-6.

131. Hutchins, "Machine Translation," pp. 93-94.

132. *Swissair News*, 19 September 1980.

133. Hutchins, "Machine Translation," p. 96-99.

134. ATA, "Profile of a Competent Translator," Ossining, n.d.

135. Ted Crump, "Translators in the Federal Government - 1984." *ATA Proceedings*, 1984.

136. P.E.N., "Manifiesto Sobre la Traducción," *Sur*, no. 338-339, 1976.

137. García Yebra, *Traducción*, pp. 349-350.

138. For a lively account of the early days of the ATA and the accreditation issue, see Bernard Bierman, *A Translator-Warrior Speaks: A personal history of the ATA, 1959-70* (Nyack: IRM, 1987) especially pp. 97-8, 152-4, 164, and 198.

139. A Spanish version of a number of the PEN papers, and the Manifesto, are to be found in *Sur*, no. 338-339, 1979.

140. Canfield, *East Meets West*, pp. 124-125.

141. Mildred Larson, "Establishing Project-Specific Criteria for Acceptability of Translations," in *American Translators Association, Translation Excellence*, ed. Marylin Gaddis Rose, (Binghampton: SUNY, 1987) pp. 69-75.

142. Edwin McDowell, "A Wizard of Words," (Rabassa). *Américas*, vol. 38, no. 4, July-August 1986, pp. 36-39.

143. *Time Magazine*, "Couriers of the Human Spirit," 19 November 1984, p. 118.

144. Personal observation, Latin American Book Fair, Washington, DC, 26 April 1986.

145. R. A. Brower, *On Translation* (N.Y.: Oxford University Press, 1966).

146. George E. Wellwarth, "Special Considerations in Drama Translation," in *Translation Spectrum*, ed. Marylin Gaddis Rose, (Binghampton: SUNY, 1981) p. 143.

SELECTED BIBLIOGRAPHY

Alfaro, President Ricardo J. *Diccionario de Anglicismos*. Madrid: Gredos, 1964.

American Translators Association. *ATA Silver Tongues*. Medford, N.J.: Learned Information, Inc.: 1984.

American Translators Association. *Translation Excellence: Assessment, Achievement, Maintenance*. Edited by Marylin Gaddis Rose, Binghampton: SUNY, 1987.

American Translators Association. *Translator and Interpreter Training and Foreign Language Pedagogy*. N.Y.: SUNY, 1989.

Arrowsmith, W. *The Craft and Context of Translation*. Austin: University of Texas Press, 1961.

Ayala, Francisco. *Problemas de la Traducción*. Madrid: Taurus, 1965.

Bassnett-McGuire, Susan. *Translation Studies*. N.Y.: Methuen, 1980.

Belloc, Hilaire. *On Translation*. Oxford: Clarendon Press, 1931.

Bly, Robert. *The Eight Stages of Translation*. Boston: Rowan, 1983.

Bower, William W. *Manual of Linguistics and Translators*. N.Y.: Scarecrow, 1959.

Brower, Reuben. *On Translation*. N.Y.: Oxford University Press, 1966.

Canfield, Lincoln. *East Meets West South of the Border*. Carbondale: Southern Illinois University Press, 1968.

Capdevila, Arturo. *Babel y el Castellano*. Buenos Aires: Losada, 1940.

Carney, Clinton C. *A Guide to Translating for the Spanish and English Bilingual*. Panama: Litografía Enan, 1988.

Catford, J.C. *A Linguistic Theory of Translation*. London: Oxford University Press, 1965.

Chacón, Luis, et al. *Bilingual Business Grammar*. Cincinnati: South-Western Publishing Co., 1981.

Congrat-Butler, Stefan. *Translations and Translators*. N.Y.: Bowker, 1979.

Crandell, T. Ellen, ed. *Translators and Translating* (Selected Essays, ATA Workshops, 1974). Binghampton: SUNY, 1974.

de la Cuesta, Leonel. *Lecciones Preliminares de Traductología*. Miami: Ediciones Guayacán, 1987.

Duff, Alan. *The Third Language: Recurrent Problems of Translation into English*. N.Y.: Pergamon Institute of English, 1981.

Ekvall, Robert. *Faithful Echo*. N.Y.: Twayne Publishers, 1960.

Escobar, Javier. *Bilingual Skills for Commerce and Industry*. Cincinnati: South-Western Publishing Co., 1984.

Felstiner, John. *Translating Neruda*. Stanford: Stanford University Press, 1980.

Frankenthaler, Marilyn. *Skills for Bilingual Legal Personnel*. Cincinnati: South-Western Publishing Co., 1982.

Frawley, William. *Translation: Literary, Linguistic and Philosophical Perspectives*. Newark: University of Delaware Press, 1984.

Fuller, Frederick. *The Translator's Handbook*. Pennsylvania State University Press, 1984.

García Yebra, Valentín. *En Torno a la Traducción*. Madrid: Gredos, 1983.

García Yebra, Valentín. *Teoría y Práctica de la Traducción*. Madrid: Gredos, 1984.

Gerrard, A. Bryson. *Cassell's Colloquial Spanish*. N.Y.: Macmillan, 1980.

Heath, Shirley Brice. *Telling Tongues: Language Policy in Mexico - Colony to Nation*. N.Y.: Columbia Teacher's College Press, 1972.

Hill, Sam. *Contrastive English-Spanish Grammatical Structures*. Lanham: University Press of America, 1985.

Holmes, James S, ed. *The Nature of Translation*. Bratislava: International Conference on Translation as an Art, 1968.

Holt, Marion. *1001 Pitfalls in Spanish*. 2nd ed., N.Y.: Barron's, 1986.

Horguelin, Paul. *Translating: a Profession*. Ottawa: Canadian Translation & Interpretation Council, 1978.

Hughes, A. Daniel. *Slang 5000 Modismos del Inglés*. Mexico: Diana: 1986.

Jakfalvi-Leiva, Susana. *Traducción, Escritura y Violencia Colonizadora: Un Estudio de la Obra del Inca Garcilaso*. Syracuse: Maxwell School of Public Affairs, 1984.

Jarvis, Ana C., et al. *Spanish for Business and Finance*. Lexington: D. C. Heath, 1988.

Kany, Charles. *American Spanish Euphemisms*. Berkeley: University of California Press, 1960.

Kelly, Louis. *The True Interpreter: a History of Translation*. Oxford: Basil, Blackwell, 1979.

Knox, Ronald A. *On English Translation*. Oxford: Oxford University Press, 1957.

Larson, Mildred. *A Manual for Problem-Solving for Bible Translation*. Grand Rapids, MI: Zondervan, 1975.

Larson, Mildred. *Meaning-Based Translation*. Lanham: University Press of America, 1984.

Labredo, Luis. *Spanish for Business and Economics*. Lexington: D.C. Heath, 1987.

Lehmann, Winifred. *Feasibility Study on Fully Automatic High Quality Translation*. University of Texas, 1971.

Manrique, Julio Colón. *Arte de Traducir el Inglés*. Mexico: Julio Colón Manrique, 1975.

Merino, Jose. *Palabras Inglesas Engañosas*. Madrid: CEEI, n.d.

Merino, Jose. *Diccionario Auxiliar del Traductor*. Madrid: CEEI, 1982.

Mosel, James N. *Embarassing Moments in Spanish how to Avoid Them*. N.Y.: Ungar, 1987.

Newmark, Peter. *Approaches to Translation*. N.Y.: Pergamon, 1982.

Nida, Eugene A. & W. D. Reyburn. *Meaning Across Cultures*. N.Y.: Orbis, 1981.

Nida, Eugene A. *Language, Structure and Translation*. Stanford: Stanford University Press, 1975.

Nida, Eugene A. *Towards a Science of Translating*. Leiden: Brill, 1964.

Olivares, Lucia Elias. *Spanish Language Use and Public Life in the U.S.*, Berlin, N.Y.: Mouton, 1985.

Orellana, Marina. *Glosario Internacional*, 2nd ed., Santiago, Chile: Calderón y Compañía, 1979.

Ortega y Gasset, José. *Miseria y Esplendor de la Traducción*. Madrid: Gredos, 1937.

Paz, Octavio. *Traducción: Literatura y Literalidad*. Barcelona: Tusqueta Editor, 1971.

PEN. *The World of Translation*. N.Y.: PEN, 1970.

Picken, Catrion. *The Translators Handbook*. London: ASLIB, 1983.

Primer Congreso Nacional de Lingüística Aplicada. *Actas*. Murcia: Universidad de Murcia, 1983.

Puerto Rico, Escuela Profesional de Traductores. *Tres Conferencias Sobre la Traducción*. San Juan: Universidad de Puerto Rico, 1971.

Puerto Rico, University Graduate Program in Translation. *Problemas de la Traducción*. San Juan, UPR, 1978.

Raffel, Burton. *The Forked Tongue: A Study of the Translation Process*. The Hague: Mouton, 1971.

Roland, Ruth A. *World Affairs*. Jefferson, N.C.: McFarland & Co., 1982.

Rose, Marilyn Gaddis, ed. *Translation Perspectives: Selected Papers*. Binghampton: SUNY, 1984.

Rose, Marilyn Gaddis, ed. *Translation Spectrum: Essays in Theory and Practice*. Albany: SUNY, 1981.

Russell, Peter. *Traducciones y Traductores en la Península Ibérica, 1400-1550*. Barcelona: Escuela Universitaria de Traductores e Intérpretes, 1985.

Savaiano, Eugene. *2001 Spanish and English Idioms*. N.Y.: Barron's Educational Series, 1976.

Savory, Theodore H. *The Art of Translation*. London: Jonathan Cape, 1968.

Schogt, Henry G. *Linguistics, Literary Analysis, and Literary Translation*. Toronto: University of Toronto Press, 1988.

Seleskovitch, Danica. *Interpreting for International Conferences*. Washington: Pen and Booth, 1978.

Shattuck, R. *The Craft and Context of Translation*. Austin: University of Texas Press, 1971.

Singleton, Charles. *Interpretation: Theory and Practice*. Baltimore: Johns Hopkins University Press, 1969.

Smith, A.H. *Aspects of Translation*. London: Secker & Warburg, 1958.

Snell-Hornby, Mary. *Translation Studies: an Integrated Approach*. Philadelphia: John Benjamins Co., 1988.

Steel, Brian. *Translation from Spanish*. Madrid: Sociedad General Española de Librería, 1979.

Steiner, George. *After Babel: Aspects of Language and Translation*. N.Y. and London: Oxford University Press, 1975.

Steiner, Roger J. *Two Centuries of Spanish and English Bilingual Lexicography (1590-1800)*. The Hague: Mouton, 1970.

Van Slype, G. *Better Translations for Better Communications*. London: Pergamon, 1983.

Vanson, George N. *Spanish-English Legal Terminology*. Cincinnati: South-Western Publishing Co., 1982.

Valdivieso, Jorge, and L. Teresa. *Negocios y Comercio*. Lexington: D.C. Heath, 1988.

Vázquez-Ayora, Gerardo. *Introducción a la Traductología*. Washington: Georgetown University Press, 1977.

Wilss, Wolfram. *The Science of Translation: An Analytical Bibliography*. Tubinger: Beitrage Zur Linguistik, 1962.

Yo-In, Song. *Translation: Theory and Practice*. Seoul: Dongguk University Press, 1975.

ABOUT THE AUTHOR

Dr Jack Child is professor of Spanish and Latin American Studies in the Department of Language and Foreign Studies of The American University, Washington, DC. He was born of American parents in Buenos Aires, Argentina, and lived in South America for 18 years before coming to the United States in 1955 to attend Yale University. Following graduation from Yale, he entered the U.S. Army, and served for 20 years as an Army Latin American Specialist until his retirement as a lieutenant colonel in 1980. His duties included translation of a wide range of materials, and interpretation for a number of senior military and civilian officials, including several chiefs of state. While on active duty he earned his Master's and Doctoral degrees in the international relations of Latin America from the School of International Service of The American University.

In 1980 he joined the School of International Service as Assistant Dean. Two years later he moved to the Department of Language and Foreign Studies, where he teaches a variety of courses (in both English and Spanish) dealing with translation, interpretation, conflict, and Latin American studies (international relations, history, art, literature).

His principal research interests have focused on conflict and its resolution in Latin America and Antarctica. He has worked with the U.S. Institute of Peace and the International Peace Academy (associated with the United Nations in New York), on issues dealing with peace-keeping and confidence-building measures in Central and South America, and has edited three books on Latin American conflict-resolution for the Academy. His interest in high latitudes has taken him to Alaska, and on six trips as staff lecturer aboard expedition cruise vessels to Antarctica and various sub-Antarctic islands, including the Malvinas/Falklands, South Georgia, and the South Orkneys.

Dr Child is a member of the American Translators Association (ATA) and the National Capital Area Chapter (Washington, DC); he is accredited by the ATA as Spanish-English and English-Spanish translator.